Easy Technology Programs for Libraries

Easy Technology Programs for Libraries

15 Quick and Popular Programs Your Patrons Will Love

David Folmar

ROWMAN & LITTLEFIELD

Lanham • Boulder • New York • London

Published by Rowman & Littlefield
A wholly owned subsidiary of The Rowman & Littlefield Publishing Group, Inc.
4501 Forbes Boulevard, Suite 200, Lanham, Maryland 20706
www.rowman.com

Unit A, Whitacre Mews, 26-34 Stannary Street, London SE11 4AB

British Library Cataloguing in Publication Information Available

Library of Congress Cataloging-in-Publication Data

Names: Folmar, David, 1969– author.
Title: Easy technology programs for libraries : 15 quick and popular programs your patrons will love / David Folmar.
Description: Lanham : Rowman & Littlefield, [2017] | Includes bibliographical references and index.
Identifiers: LCCN 2017018650 (print) | LCCN 2017040005 (ebook) | ISBN 9781442277502 (electronic) | ISBN 9781442277496 (pbk. : alk. paper)
Subjects: LCSH: Libraries and adult education. | Information technology—Study and teaching. | Internet literacy—Study and teaching. | Social media. | Online social networks.
Classification: LCC Z718.8 (ebook) | LCC Z718.8 .F65 2017 (print) | DDC 025.5—dc23
LC record available at https://lccn.loc.gov/2017018650

∞™ The paper used in this publication meets the minimum requirements of American National Standard for Information Sciences—Permanence of Paper for Printed Library Materials, ANSI/NISO Z39.48-1992.

Printed in the United States of America

Contents

Preface

Librarians are under pressure to offer computer and technology classes. While there may seem to be plenty of established classes available, these are primarily designed for the beginner or novice user. Few classes go further than teaching elementary job skills or social-media aptitude. After 15 years of libraries and schools offering these classes, most of our patrons know the basics. They need someone to help them learn additional computer skills that will positively affect their lives. However, discovering these skills and learning how to do them takes time. It is time patrons do not have. For librarians, time is spent learning patron needs and vetting websites and applications to fill them; time the general librarian does not have. And not all librarians have had the opportunity to advance their own computer skills much beyond that of their patrons.

For small rural or suburban libraries, this can prove especially problematic. Once a library offers basic classes, there is no way to further develop digital education unless it invests in a more specialized staff member and facilities like maker spaces or dedicated computer labs. While it may seem ideal to invest in these, it competes with budgeting for traditional library services, or takes away from providing the services that the community has come to expect and love.

This book is for those libraries that do not have dedicated staff to offer computer programs beyond introductory classes. It provides 15 step-by-step programs, using free online software, that go beyond the introduction to computer basics, and provides you, the librarian, with all you need for classes that engage your community in the use of computers. The focus of the book is not on job skills, or enterprise software like Word and Access. Instead, it takes an individual user's objective and provides a computer-based answer.

The objectives these programs are designed to solve are real-world problems and interests that I have encountered with my patrons, friends, and family. The solutions to these problems are designed around free-to-use shareware, websites, and open source software, in part because the cost is right for a small library program, but also because these programs will enable patrons to solve their problems without new associated costs. Also important is the fact that the premise of *Easy Technology Programs* is a low-cost-of-entry digital solution to a problem, both in terms of the low financial cost and the low cost in skill and training, and will encourage a deeper digital literacy in your patrons.

Compared to other works on technology classes, the projects are geared toward the average staff skill level, with step-by-step instructions, and are designed to make both the technology and teaching approach easier. While other books may only focus on programs, this book also focuses on the teaching process. All too often librarians are called on to teach, and it is not always comfortable for them to do so. So, the programs give advice on how to teach and how to encourage interaction between patrons. More than a lecture, the programs are workshops for helping patrons successfully explore new possibilities offered by digital technology, together and as a community.

In addition, many books focus on a particular program in the hopes that the librarian has patrons who would find that program to be useful. Instead of teaching a possibly useful skill, this book focuses on library patrons who have a specific project, but cannot afford to hire someone to complete the project for them. The classes will identify patrons' needs and teach them where to acquire certain apps, or show them websites and how to use them effectively. For instance, Google Voice can be used to create a virtual office that allows patrons to separate their private from their professional contact information. Or, Sweet Home 3D is a program that can be used by homeowners or contractors to create modifiable layouts of rooms, export images, and make a virtual walkthrough. It is easy to use, free, and helps people visualize home renovations. By encouraging the use of computers for personal activities, we encourage digital literacy.

The basis for this approach is knowing that people who excel in the field of information technology (IT) were often coming to technology because their interest is based on their personal, rather than professional, life. Tech people were not using computers at home because they were good with computers; rather, they were good with computers because they were using them at home. The home use could cover anything from being a computer hobbyist, or an avid video gamer, or even using computers to sell items online. People used computers to meet their needs, and seemed to be successful using them for work as well. The Montessori method, which uses what they call a "discovery model," reinforces this premise. In essence, the discovery model suggests that students will learn concepts from working with materials, in this case software and computers, rather than from our traditional top-down model of providing answers.

A perfect example of digital literacy in a negative sense is the "digital divide" problem. Children in households with computers tend to learn digital skills quicker than children in households where there is no computer. One might think that the problem is not having access to a computer, but schools teach students the digital skills. It is having time to use computers that is the problem. How do you motivate people to use computers? You let them solve their problems on a computer. I give examples of a problem to solve in each program in this book, but I will start with one I don't mention in any of the programs: my own son.

One day, I found my son walking through lines of Java code looking for one syntax error. He had downloaded and remodified a Minecraft mod that he could not get to run correctly. The thought of my son, whom I could barely get to focus for the 20 minutes it takes to clean his room, poring over code for a period of several hours was pretty jarring. Having worked with programmers and done a small amount of programming myself, I knew what a mind-bogglingly boring task this could be. It struck me that the simple fact that he *wanted* to do this was the powerful motivator. He had ownership of the problem and its solution. I realized that the reason so many children and grandchildren became the domestic IT departments of their families was because kids, and some older adults, started by doing what they *wanted* to do, not necessarily what they *needed* to do.

So, rather than create a book based around a "big idea" in digital literacy or job skills, this book offers a series of answers to possible problems your patrons will have. If the presenter knows and can fill in the "big concepts," that is good, but if not, that is also good. Rather than trying to teach skills, we are focusing on getting patrons involved with technology. The book is not meant to be a teaching guide to computer literacy; the book is simply a resource for librarians to help patrons engage with technology to solve their own problems.

The book includes:

- 15 quick, easy classes focused on actual outcomes for patrons, without requiring a budget, dedicated facilities, or specialized knowledge.
- Programs that your patrons can relate to—geared toward actual needs or interests, and not just geared toward "techy" people.

Each program includes:

- How-tos and other elements to help patrons effectively use simple software and allow them to get optimal results from their effort.
- Step-by-step instructions to enable the average computer user to teach patrons with ease and authority.
- Tips on how instructors can engage their audience and not lose patrons to information overload.
- Reasons and rationale behind the creation of the classes, so that instructors can modify a class for their own patrons' needs and tastes.

You are given all the tools you need as a presenter to show relatable uses of technology, and to make sure that patrons can see the possibilities in using the software. Step-by-step instructions are focused on patrons leaving with practical skills for everyday life using freely available resources such as YouTube, eBay, Google, and Indeed.

Acknowledgments

Thank you to the wonderful Lorraine Waltz for everything. Auggie and Ellie, I thank you. Thank you, Rebecca, Judy, and Ingrid, each in turn. Thank you, Patty Parks, for something to do with libraries. Thank you, Delta, and thank you, Lynn, for proving that library assistants are smarter than librarians, at least one anyhow, and being nice to him. And finally, thank you to you, for reading this.

Introduction

Digital Literacy and Libraries

Someone wants you to teach computer classes—your manager, your director, the library board, or your community. If they didn't, you wouldn't be looking at this book. If you're like me, you have taught the basics. An introduction to computers, a class on email for beginners, and a mix of social media classes are low-hanging fruit. It is easy to find resources to run these courses. But after you teach them, what next? What do you teach when the community asks, "What comes next?" If the library's goal in offering computer classes is to make people "digitally literate," have we accomplished that? What does "digitally literate" even mean?

Paul Gilster, in his book *Digital Literacy*, gives the definition as "The ability to understand and use information in multiple formats from a wide range of sources when it is presented via computers."[1] To a librarian, this makes sense, as this is information literacy as applied to digital technology. The definition is pretty close to what we learned in library school. So, does this mean that we teach information literacy? Well, I have tried that route. Some of my first classes offered deep web searching, and security and cryptography primers. I can say that I (at least) did not find an audience.

The classes consisted of me, just myself and a couple of handouts waiting in an empty room. So, moving to more theoretical classes didn't seem to be what my public library patrons were interested in. I was also teaching the basics at the time, and noticed that when I worked distributed networks and cloud concepts into email classes, my patrons liked it. They responded to information when I could relate it to something for which they had a little understanding. They were also interested when I explained that computers bounce an email around between servers, and how Gmail is really a cloud for email. Google just took those attachments and made it possible to edit them online, since the company had to store them on the server anyhow. This is the cloud, enabling editing of attachments on Google computers. This helped patrons understand and made them more comfortable. My patrons were interested in concepts—just not ones they did not use.

So, the first question for libraries is: How do we address providing other classes that focus on actual needs? Some libraries have had luck with moving into teaching more basic skills, like Microsoft Office, but not all libraries can do this. Part of the problem is resources; how do you "teach" Microsoft Office at a library? High school and colleges cover Microsoft Office in a semester-length class. Even breaking it down to Word, Excel, PowerPoint, and other products means you will have a series of classes—classes offered by high schools, colleges, Goodwill job programs, some state unemployment offices, and continuing education programs.

This is not to say that these classes are not worth teaching, and many libraries do. These libraries also have the staff who use and teach these products. How many library systems are lucky enough to be able to afford that much time and resources to teaching these courses? Is this where you want to invest your resources, when the classes teaching these skills are offered by other organizations and are competing for your patrons? Do we *need* to be teaching these classes?

We are left with the question: What is the library trying to do, and how does it do this differently, using the resources available to us? Again, the idea behind these classes is making people "digitally literate," but how do we teach someone to be "digitally literate"?

Cornell University's definition of digital literacy, "The ability to find, evaluate, utilize, share, and create content using information technologies and the Internet,"[2] is close to what we need to work toward in terms of digital literacy in libraries. The functional difference is "create content." As I see it, the difference between Gilster's version of digital literacy and the Cornell University definition is how to understand information via computer. When we help people create, disseminate, and use computers for information and communication, we focus on actually *doing* things, and open up learning from there.

Teaching email and Facebook and web pages means that you're teaching patrons how to log on to other machines and accounts. The web pages "live" on other machines, and users simply use their own machines (or the library's) to look into the files saved there. Now patrons start to understand distributed networks, and the Internet, and client-server relationships. Teaching patrons why user IDs and passwords are needed to create an account is a way to explain the basics of unique identifiers and databases. So how do we teach these big concepts? We teach patrons what they want to learn, and incorporate the bigger idea into the lesson. The ideas behind digital literacy are easier to understand when they are being applied.

The classes outlined in this book are about giving patrons reasons to use a computer beyond passive consumption of media. Some of these programs are a little on the frivolous side, I admit it. However, using the computer helps users to *understand* the computer. A wonderful tool, the "Mousing Around" mouse tutorial created by the Palm Beach County Library System (http://pbclibrary.org/mousing/), which is based on the "New User Tutorial" created by The Library Network of Michigan (http://tln.lib.mi.us/tutor/), was in some sense my inspiration for this approach. Other instructors have shared with me that it is hard to teach Microsoft Office products when people can barely right-click a mouse. Instead of divorcing the action of using a computer from understanding it, the library made it a game. Palm Beach even provides games requiring mouse skills to "gamify" mouse use. Patrons must work the interface a little before jumping up to learning more skills. The tutorial demonstrates the idea that patrons must want to do the work, and the instructors just teach them what they are doing. This is basically the rule of thumb that I follow for computer workshops.

Or in other words:

- Use empowers understanding
- Employ objective-based learning
- Teach the interface, not the program

Let us break these out.

RULE OF THUMB 1: USE EMPOWERS UNDERSTANDING

Some people are going to hate the idea that any computer use is good use. They will think of "gamers," or the ingrained narcissism of social media. However, everyone needs to start someplace and, after the basics, will need something more intermediate. To put this in library-speak, in the same way juvenile fiction leads to young adult novels, which lead (theoretically) to literature, games and social media can pave the way to these classes, and then (theoretically) information literacy.

As I stated earlier, something as simple as Facebook (FB) can teach the idea behind linked data and metatags. So base your classes on activities, and fit in any big concepts that you know. Some of these concepts are included in the classes, and I expect you to have some understanding of them. But don't worry if you don't, as knowing these concepts is not as important to teaching these classes as giving the patrons hands-on time on machines.

In my own and others' experience, it is hard to teach Office when people can barely right-click. Patrons need to work the interface a little before jumping up to learning more skills. We don't need to make people "digitally" literate, but simply move them in that direction by helping them acquire a better understanding of computers. Patrons need to have reasons to use computer skills.

RULE OF THUMB 2: EMPLOY OBJECTIVE-BASED LEARNING

This leads me to my next point, objective based learning, which is from the maker movement. Like many working in libraries, I have been following the maker movement for a while. When we run out to buy a Makey Makey or Arduino, an aspect that is overlooked by some people is the fact that the maker movement was based on practicality. The movement never set out to teach STEM (science, technology, engineering, and math) skills. While it is fun to make robots, one of the original ideas of the maker movement is the concept of owning an object by making it. Mark Frauenfelder, editor-in-chief of *Make* magazine, wrote *Made by Hand: Searching for Meaning in a Throwaway World* (2010), which was an early inspiration for the maker movement. One of my favorite projects that Frauenfelder talks about is a wooden spoon.

The idea behind making is creating meaningful objects. The relationship to the object you are making is as important as the impetus to make it. This leads to my second "rule." In my experience, patrons use computers because they need to, not because they have a great desire to know more about computers. They are taking these classes to achieve something. If we build classes around their objectives, we can do a better job getting them interested in computers and helping them become more digitally literate.

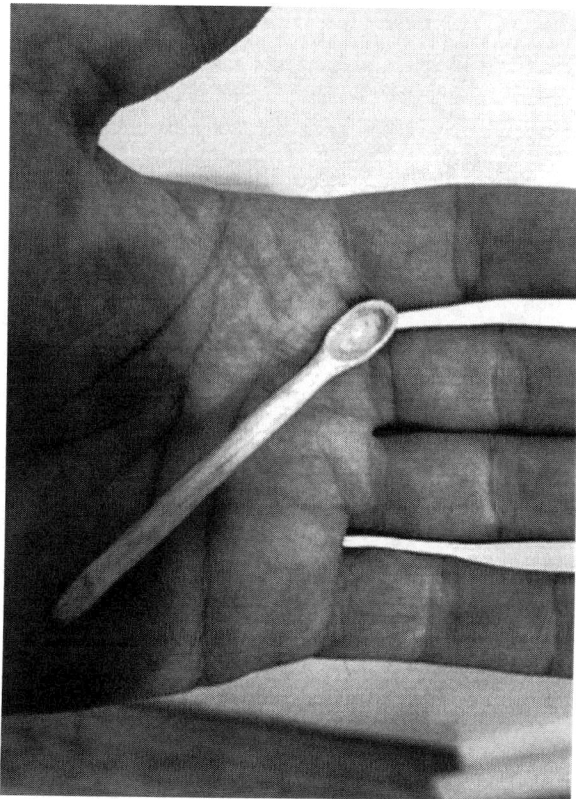

The spoon is a useful object. ***Project: Wooden Salt Cellar, Make, 2011. Retrieved December 7, 2016, from http://makezine.com/2011/11/14/project_wooden_salt_cellar/***

The mail icon

The save icon

The folder icon

If I ran a class on JPEG versus PNG resolution, I don't think many people would come. But a class on more colorful pictures for Facebook and better-looking text on Instagram might get some takers. Of course, I would be teaching the same thing; it is just how the information will be used. For instance, I never taught Microsoft Word, but I did teach some classes on making a resume. I threw away the Word templates and replaced them with rich-text format templates for Open Office. I told the patrons that they could make a resume in in Microsoft Word, and change it in Google Docs. In that class, I covered not just Word, but all text editors, and also taught a little about open source format. The participants did not learn a "digital skill"; they learned how to make a resume, and they learned more about computers that could be applied more broadly

RULES OF THUMB 3: TEACH THE INTERFACE, NOT THE PROGRAM

By "teach the interface," I mean explain what the program is doing, and how it relates to the objective. When teaching classes, I wondered: How did I understand computers, and how do millennials understand them? How is their understanding different from how we are teaching them? Luckily, I am an old man and remember things, like what the icons on page xiii originally meant.

These indicate Send mail, Save, and Folder, respectively. How many teens know these, and have actually sent a letter using a floppy disk, or even a manila envelope? I would hazard not too many, yet they recognize the icons and can use them from program to program. Certainly, at one point someone explained these images to them, but the consistency is what makes these work. When aspects of an interface change, either due to the program being updated or adoption of a new program, some things keep the same functions as a program we are familiar with. In the examples above, every program saves actions. It might not employ a floppy disk; it might instead have a button labeled save. Either way, an experienced user can usually figure out what to do to make it work, because enough is similar rather than different.

There is a consistency across programs. Icons are a great example of something that flows between programs, but there are other elements as well: logos as home buttons, drop-down menus, how a radio button works. Computer programs are designed to be easy to use by people. If you understand what a computer is doing when you use a program, you can start to make assumptions and learn more about computers and digital processes in general. When you as the instructor click on Save, explain that you are saving; don't just say click on the floppy before closing. The backup file is useful if the computer crashes or if you want to get the file again at a later date.

If you want to walk into bigger issues, explain that you are creating a local backup, and that every program does that. If possible, always use the Save As command, which will call up the interface with file structure, so that you can explain *where* the file is being saved in a computer folder. Beyond basics like saving, these classes offer low-level programs for doing things for which there are more expensive versions. For example, there is a class on PhotoCat (program 2). PhotoCat is a fairly low-level photo editor, but it uses the same language as Photoshop. If you teach students to use the Contrast key, and look under the menu from time to time, then they will have a better grasp if they move on to more "serious software." If you want to explain what contrast is, that would be even better. If you can explain how the gray tones are pushed more toward black or white, this is even better; not everyone will get that, but by using the button they will. In this way, I believe that these easy classes are a good step between grasping the basics and advanced digital literacy.

HOW TO USE THESE PROGRAMS

Let's move on to the practical aspect of this book: How do you use these classes? My suggestion is to run one or two programs a month, in rotation. If you're in a library system, you can run quite a few programs per branch. The idea here is to not burn out your patron base by overusing people interested in these topics. If you run 15 of these in a month, no one will show up the third month. Also pay attention to your patrons; some topics or programs may not jibe with them, but you may run into another use for these programs.

So be flexible when teaching the programs. In some cases, I discovered these programs as I was researching something else. Podcasting, which is also useful for oral histories, is an example; another is Google Voice for home businesses or even homeless patrons. PhotoCat could be part of four of the programs in the book, as well as work as a stand-alone class. Likewise, there are often alternative computer programs mentioned. I cannot go over every computer program, but the structure and goals can be approached using different software, maybe one that you would be more comfortable teaching. The flexibility of having several options and knowing more than one is also important, because a downside of using free software is that the interface can change in an update.

WHY SO MUCH SELF-PROMOTION IN THE CLASSES?

When you read through these programs, I often refer to ways to use social media or ways to create a partnership to promote the program. This is because libraries seem to have a problem entering the field of technology. We have a certain reputation, one that is being fought, but we have it nonetheless. Some of the "big guns" out there, like the New York Public Library and the Fayetteville Free Library, are doing great work with technology promotion, but there are a lot of little guys hacking away at the problem too. These smaller library systems must constantly fight the misconception, both external and internal, that libraries are still just about books.

Remember, promotion is not mandatory; indeed, some of you may be working with marketing departments that are not all that keen on you doing their job. However, marketing is hard and scary work in its own way, and if you talk to someone in those departments, he or she might like the help or have some great ideas to help you. Listen to your marketers, and get their help. You have the same goal, and if they say no, it is because sometimes, good intentions and a sense of humor don't translate across mediums.

FINALLY, IT NEVER HURTS TO ASK

You might think, wow, I need to be an expert in all these concepts to teach these classes. I am not an expert; instead, I was very lucky to have made some great friends and acquaintances over the years—DJs, social media marketers, even patrons who just "got it" and were not afraid to help out. Some of my programs are based on classes that others ran originally, and I just helped and learned from them. These people gave me ideas and input; listening and trying these projects will help you know more about computers, the same way it helps the patrons. I learned more from the kids in my LAN gaming club about setting up a local server than from people I knew in IT. Look outside the library for ideas and help; you never know where it will come from. We are, after all, an institution about finding knowledge: in books, online, or in people.

NOTES

1. Paul Gilster, *Digital Literacy* (New York: Wiley and Computer Publishing, 1997), 1.
2. Cornell University Digital Literacy Resource, "Digital Literacy Is . . ." n.d. https://digitalliteracy.cornell.edu/.

Part I

PROGRAMS FOR THE CREATIVE LIFESTYLE

The focus of these five workshops is community. The history of the public library in America starts with Benjamin Franklin and the Library Company of Philadelphia. This library, while not a public library in the sense we have come to know it, was the first library for public use that was not attached or sponsored by a larger organization. It would be a few decades until a local government sponsored a library for its community; however, the ideals behind this library were a major influence until the Andrew Carnegie era.

Founded by the Junto Society, the library held works on economics, solving social woes, politics, and science. Its motto was "To support the common good is divine"; in other words, libraries are for the common good, the good of the community and its people.

A library's success is in the new things and ideas it brings to the community it serves. How we measure success is how people change the world, not succeed in this one. So, when we look for ways to support the communities we live in, it is not always necessary to do anything other than just improve the "quality of life of patrons."

From Facebook to Face-to-Face

Facebook or Meetup for Family Reunions/Meetings

WHY BOTHER?

We can assume your patrons are on Facebook (abbreviated FB hereafter). They are using it to share memes, post messages, and share links with each other. Corporations and organizations use social media to create awareness of a product or bring people together for a cause. Your patrons can use social media the same way for their organization, club, or just holding a family event. FB pages will help them spread the word, keep track of the people attending, and notify those people of activities leading up to their event and following it, taking their social media skills to the next level.

We will use FB as an illustration, and talk about Meetup. The positive side of FB is that it is free, and it can leverage a library patron's existing social networks and the social networks of those who are invited and attend an event. Meetup benefits the patron when he or she must reach a wider audience outside his or her social network, but wants to control the number of attendees. Meetup has other benefits, like attracting people interested in a subject but are not part of a social circle. Meetup allows patrons to reach people they do not know and grow a new community. Also, Meetup's ticketing feature can put a limit on attendees, a handy feature when a group is meeting in, say, a library meeting room that only holds 50 people.

WHAT PATRONS WILL NEED

- Basic computer skills
- An email account
- A Facebook account
- An event they want to promote or host

WHAT YOU WILL NEED

- An open Internet connection that allows social media
- A premade Facebook account for an organization or cause, and/or a Meetup account
- Ability to display an active computer screen (projector monitor, or enough room for everyone to gather around)
- A reason for making a new Event page
- A description, time, and place for the event
- A nice graphic to promote the event, in a proper format

OUTLINE

1. Find Events on your FB page
2. Walk patrons through creating an Event page
3. Have them set up an FB Event page
4. Help them create a description, include an image for their event, and categorize a public event
5. Show patrons how to invite attendees, how attendees can invite new people, and how FB Groups can be used to speed up the process
6. Show them how to update an event and post on the event timeline, and explain how they can increase attendance.
7. Go over how Meetup can be used in comparison.

THE BIG PICTURE

This project covers in detail how to set up an FB event page, explain what patrons need to make it useful and attractive, and show how to invite people to join.

Also covered are best practices for making sure that people attend. The class also covers how Meetup can be used. What does Meetup offer that is different from FB, and how can a patron manage those differences? As a paid option, Meetup is less likely to be interesting to patrons with limited computer knowledge or use. However, because it could be a better option, we can at least help them decide if it is for them.

CLASS

Find Events on Your FB Page

The first step in this class will be to create an Event page in front of your patrons. We want to give them an overview of the process, and help them understand how it functions. To do this, you will need to have an account already established that you don't mind sharing with your patrons in the class. If you have a personal FB account and do not mind displaying its content, that could work. A better solution is to have access to your library's FB account. If you have this kind of access, you can use it to make a page for an upcoming program.

> **PRO TIP**
>
> **In the class, show patrons how to invite attendees, and how to share the event with others. If you create an actual upcoming event at your library, you can invite the patrons to it and ask them to share it with their social network. It is a chance to promote another upcoming class or event. It would not be mandatory for them, but it is always helpful to promote where you can.**

If you do not have that access to your library system social media, think of using a FB page created for just your branch. Another option is a page for your Library Friends group (with their permission). The Friends option is especially useful if your group promotes and funds events. These options are nice because the event is relevant and helps promote your library. However, if you have an existing social media policy or strategy, don't be surprised if your marketing department or team prefers you don't use an actual event.

And if all these options are not viable, there is one more. We talked about using your own personal page, which you may not want to do. You can create a personal page that is not yours, under an alias for someone at the library. The benefit of this personal alias account is that it looks more like the pages the patrons probably use, which creates less opportunity for confusion when you show them how to make an event.

FB has rather strict terms of services; they want pages *only* for *real* people or organizations. That being said, there may be a staff member who would not mind using his or her email account to create a personal page. Although FB requires you be a "real person," many people use an alias on FB, which is not against the terms of service. So using a staff member's email does not mean his or her name or likeness must be attached to that FB account.

When you have an account to use, show your patrons the steps to create an Event page. Take the patrons through the following steps.

1. Select the Home or Timeline/Profile page of your FB account.
2. To the right of the Search box is your account button. It will have your profile picture and name. Clicking on this will take you to a page that has the information of the profile, and the timeline.
3. The background picture in FB is the image that sits at the top of the page behind the profile pic. Across the bottom of the background pic is another toolbar. It should be in this order: Timeline, About, Friends, Photos, More.
4. The Arrow after More is what we want to click. Click on it and a drop-down menu will appear. On this menu is the Events option.
5. Click on Events. The Timeline should disappear and the items under the cover photo should change to a list of all the events the person or place in the profile has been associated with. They will be either events they were invited to or held. At the top is a button to create an event.
6. It is pretty hard to miss. Click on this button and you should get the Create Event pop-up.

Walk Patrons Through Creating an Event Page

We are now ready to enter event information. Some of this information cannot be changed after the fact, so this is a good time to check with your patrons if they have their information ready. Make sure that when you are actually helping them make pages, they have their information ready, or at least have thought about it so they can choose whether or not to fill certain options, or enter them later.

> **PRO TIP**
>
> **Before a class, create your event description and images. Have them ready in a Microsoft Word or other document. Copy and paste this into FB as you create the live page.**

More importantly, it will help break up the class and give patrons a chance to talk, so it is not just lecturing. Taking a moment to get patrons to talk prevents information overload, so that they don't start losing interest. In addition, this is a good practice because it lets them share not just with you, but with each other, strengthening the sense of community in your library and classes.

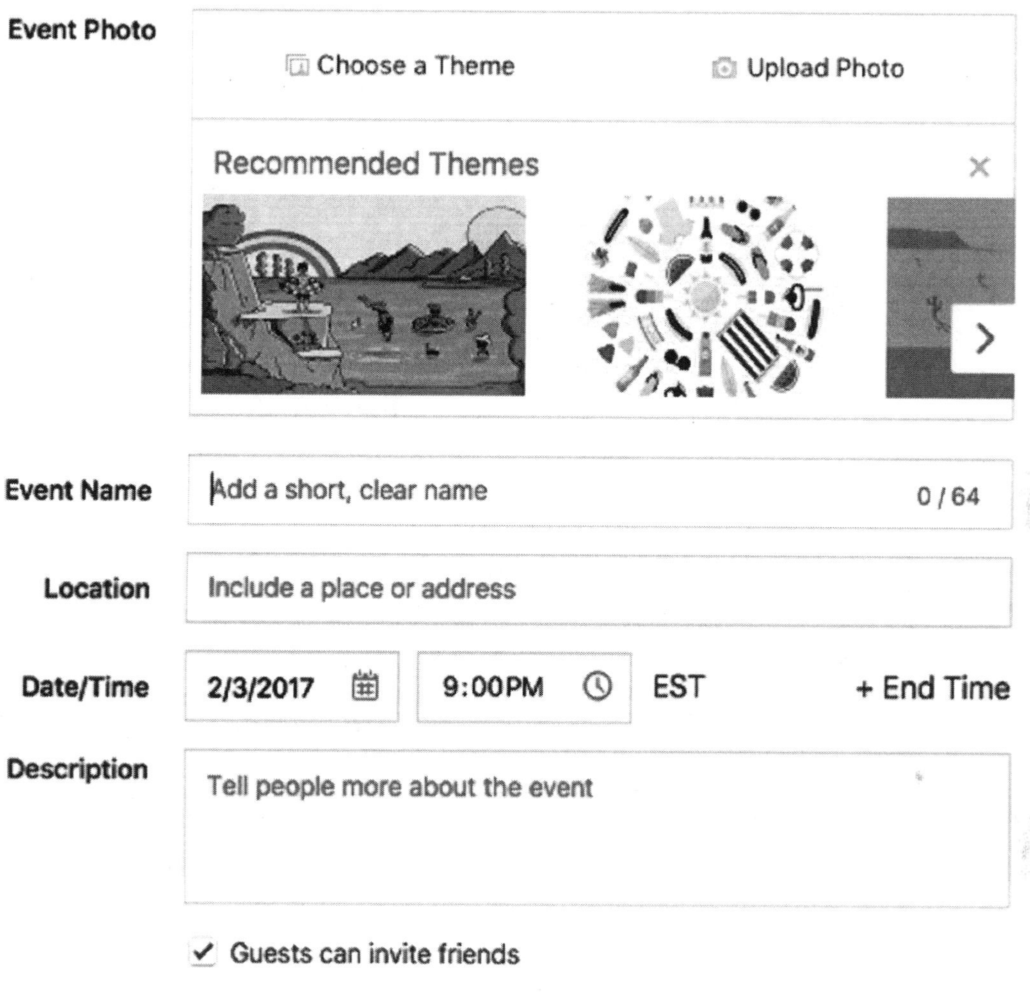

The Facebook event creation interface defines the what, when, and where of your meeting.

> **PRO TIP**
>
> **As the patrons explain their event, keep the class moving. If they start to go into too much detail, ask someone else in the class what they think, and then talk about their project.**

Now go over the event checklist—ask patrons if they have these things, and let them share theirs to the extent of their comfort level. Hopefully they will be excited by the opportunity. The event checklist includes:

1. Name of event
2. Time of event
3. Location of event
4. Is it public or private?

5. Image to use for event (program 11 in this book covers finding images online without breaking copyright, and may be useful for this)

If patrons have all this information and you have a text editor like Word on the computer, ask them to write it in Word now. If the patrons do not have all the information, then you can help them set up a "dummy" page. Setting up the page is just to help them feel comfortable with the process. The information can be edited later in the same interface used to create an event.

Set Up an FB Event Page

The first step is creating an event, and deciding if it will be public or private. If it is private, the patron will simply add the information we have asked for. It can be filled out in the Open Dialogue box. Once they are done, the event is created. It is simple as that. They can then can go ahead and write in, or copy and paste the description. If they are doing a public event, the situation is a little more difficult. The major difference between the private and public event page is that it can be "found" and "searched" through FB.

Ask the patron creating a private event to bear with you. To get a sense of what kind of public events are available, type a subject in the search box at the top of the FB page—knitting, for example. The Search box is next to the FB logo in the upper-right corner. When you search your term, a new menu appears directly under the normal blue header. Across the top is a series of categories to refine the search. The last item is Events.

Refine the search by choosing Events from the top. Ask the patrons to search for meetings similar to theirs. It is possible they may have been thinking of starting a club, and there is one in their area already.

> **PRO TIP**
>
> **Public events will require a host. It must be a Public page, and patrons will need to have administering rights to it. If the patrons already have a club page they may use it; if not, it might be nice to set up an FB page for the library class. The library class page can also be used to promote classes in the library like this one. Let patrons create that event under your account if they are meeting in the library. You can also create a dummy account to create this event.**

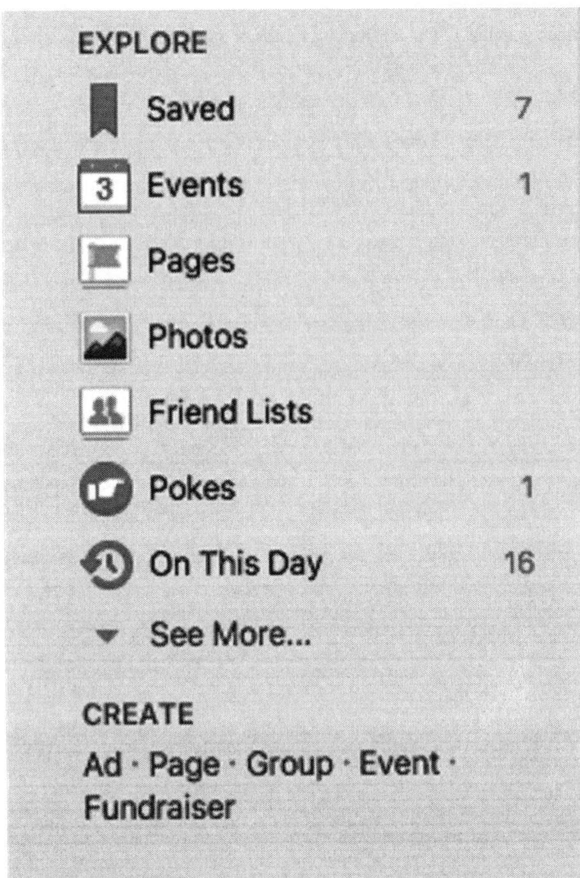

On the FB menu to the left, you will find the Create options, including events.

This search will bring up all public events in the area, and patrons can see how they are broken down by category and location.

To get a better sense of what is available in your area, navigate to the News Feed page. In case you do not know, News Feed page is the main page usually seen when logging onto FB. On the left is a series of options in a menu, as shown in the figure above. Under Explore you will find Events again.

Click on Events from your News Feed. When the new Events Feed opens, there are two items of interest: Location and Categories. The Location will be in the main feed and will say Events near [your town]. The Categories is the last item in the feed, so you may have to scroll down. Categories include:

- Arts
    - Art
    - Books
    - Film
- Causes
    - Fundraisers
    - Volunteering

- Community
  - Family
  - Festivals
  - Neighborhoods
  - Religious
  - Shopping
- Entertainment
  - Comedy
  - Concerts
  - Dance Performance
  - Night Life
  - Theater
- Food and Drink
  - Dining
  - Tasting
- Interests
  - Conference
  - Meetup
- Learning
  - Classes
  - Talk
  - Workshops
- Sports and Fitness
  - Fitness
  - Sports and Games

FB categories are more limited than those in Meetup. When you start a book club, for instance, you will need to use keywords if you want to specify a book club specifically for mysteries. So, Category will be Art—Book, and you will use the keyword Mystery. It is searchable by keyword, but it is also advisable to put that term in the Description, if not the title. Take this opportunity to say that the class will look at that at the end of the class.

PRO TIP

To librarians, FB provides a fairly weak taxonomy. For instance, our knitting club would most likely be placed under Interests—Meet Up and use the keyword Knitting. At the end of this chapter there is more about the taxonomy of Meetup and how it is preferable.

You can now show your patrons how to create an event. The Create Event opens dialogue in a drop-down menu located in the upper-right corner. You can specify Public or Private. For Private, the information needed is what you asked for earlier: Event Photo, Event Name, Location, Date/Time, and Description (where you will place the description the patrons discussed). There is one more option you did not discuss; under the Description text box is a check box. It will allow the event planner to check whether guests can invite people. The patrons need to remember that they will not be able to limit the number. It can easily get out of hand if they have limited room and resources.

Explain that if patrons choose this option, it will allow all guests, and guests of guests to invite people, so use it sparingly.

When you choose Public, the interface changes, offering more options. Here are the Public Event options:

- An FB Public Event must specify an Event Host. The available options for the Event Host are to the right of the dialogue options. These include any FB account linked to the FB account under which you are logged in. So, if you're a moderator of group pages, that should show up in the drop-down menu. For privacy reasons, if nothing else, patrons should use a public club page to create a Public Event page. If the patron does not have one, it might be necessary to create a public page.
- Basic Info is for the same information you would fill in on a Private Event dialogue.
- Details is where you specify the categories they explored earlier and add a description. There is also a check box for Free Admission and for Family Friendly.
- Tickets will allow you to link to Event Brite or another ticketing platform.
- Options will let the patron moderate the content. You can invite other FB users to cohost, limit who can post on the Event page, and choose whether to display a guest list.

When you bring up the Ticketing option, it is a good time to discuss the ability to use Meetup as an alternative to FB Event pages. It has ticketing built in, meaning you can limit the number of attendees and create waiting lists. It also allows more categorization and creates a meeting notification for people who have joined and are looking for events in that category. The drawback of Meetup is the fact that it is a *for pay* service.

Now walk your patrons through setting up the Event page, including classifications, and help them set up the page.

PRO TIP

If you use your library's FB page or, better yet, your class FB page to host events, Administrator approval for posts is necessary to keep family-friendly content on the site.

Creating Descriptions and Including Images for Events

With FB's limitations on categories, the pressure is on your patrons to "sell" the event with descriptions and images. Descriptions should probably be three or four detailed sentences about what is going to happen. You want to cover what the event is about, and who is invited. For instance, it is important to state that a seniors' class is for retirees or those over 55 years of age at the beginning of the description, if that is who you want for the event. It is also important that you mention exactly what you are planning on doing. Remember, this is going to the public; the less confusion, the better the experience.

You can help patrons make this as attractive an event as possible, but writing copy is a tricky business. Since there is no limitation to the length of the description, they can add as much as they want. However, the best approach is to help the patrons hit the high points and add details afterward.

The other important part of making an Event page attractive is the image. For a Private Event, there are themes available for the image. You will notice them at the top when you create the Event page. For the most part, these themes can be used for the class, and images can always be added and edited later. If the patron is making a Public Event page, explain that images are more important in that case, and suggest they choose an image. FB can be very picky about images; they should be exactly 1920 by 1080 pixels. FB will crop things oddly if they are not. At the very least, you need to keep the aspect ratio or width-to-height ratio consistent, and the image larger.

It may be necessary to load an image of 1920 by 1920 pixels when you do create the Event, as FB will sometimes default to a square image for mobile devices. Remember, it is always better to scale down rather than up, but if all possible, use the 1920 by 1080 pixel image.

Show Patrons How to Invite Attendees

When creating an Event page, the final step for either type of page is to invite people. Inviting people is very easy; under the Event image on the right-hand side is

PRO TIP

Show your patrons how to use the Google Image search and refine by size (and usage). You can usually get some Creative Commons (CC) images from Google Images in a size that is acceptable. If you need to crop the image, parts of program 11 on image manipulation in this book can be used for this class.

an Invite button. Simply click on the list, and it will pull up a dialogue box. This dialogue will allow the creator to invite any FB friends they have, as well as people in their contact list of email associated with their FB account. If you want to invite someone not on your contact list, you can simply type in their email or cell phone number and text them. For a Public Event page, anyone invited or who discovers the event and says they will attend can invite people.

NOTES ABOUT MEETUP

Why would your patrons select Meetup as compared to FB? It has an associated fee, is not as recognizable, and does not have as many users as FB. Both FB and Meetup will allow you to create a page for the meeting and for the group. Both can be used as a place for attendees and organizers to talk to each other. Attendees can also start dialogues about the events. Meetup also has some nice features for calendars for Group or Club events, but to be honest, it is not much different from what FB does. (It is worth mentioning that Meetup was around first, and many of the features of FB events seem to be inspired by Meetup.) So, patrons must be willing to spend money on Meetup. Choosing this option comes down to two factors:

1. Ticketing: The ticketing is the more obviously useful factor. If you have a limited number of possible attendees, Meetup will let you give out tickets on a first-come, first-served basis. It will also allow waiting lists, and will automatically contact attendees about the changes to the event or if a ticket becomes available.
2. Searchability: While seemingly less obvious, searchability is potentially more useful. When a person signs up for Meetup, they choose their interests. FB events are driven primarily by geography or direct contact. The Meetups have a larger number of categories.

∞ **All Meetups**

Meetups with friends

Arts & Culture

Book Clubs

Career & Business

Cars & Motorcycles

Community & Environment

Dancing

Education & Learning

Fashion & Beauty

Fitness

Food & Drink

Games

Health & Wellbeing

Hobbies & Crafts

Language & Ethnic Identity

LGBT

Lifestyle

Movements & Politics

Movies & Film

Music

New Age & Spirituality

Outdoors & Adventure

Paranormal

Parents & Family

Pets & Animals

Photography

Religion & Beliefs

Sci-Fi & Fantasy

Singles

Socializing

Sports & Recreation

Support

Tech

Writing

Meetup provides categories that people can follow to find your events, or be notified when you make one that matches their preferences.

Users can identify which categories they are interested in based on their interests, and a gathering that fits that bill will be identified and suggested they log in. Categorization creates two factors to reach new members: one helps users who are specifically interested in the subject of the meeting, and the second helps those actively looking for a gathering. In combination, it makes the categorization a factor worth considering.

How the Topic Came Up and Became a Class

Richmond Public Library tried to keep FB Events pages for all our major events. We wanted to create them for all meetings. The sheer number of meetings made this impossible for one or two of us to keep up with it. I first went through the steps to create a guide for other librarians and staff. Then I crafted it for outside organizations that hold meetings in our public spaces. Finally, needing some new programs, I changed it so that the program could be used for all patrons who may wish to try their hand at creating events.

PRO TIP

If your library has meeting rooms, you should consider Meetup and offering its use to the organizations using the library. It is a good barometer of the interests of your community and the number of people who are actively trying to meet. It is an easy way to get programs and people in the door.

Making Pictures Perfect with PhotoCat

Easy Online Photo Editing

WHY BOTHER?

Everyone has a phone camera and is taking pictures. Still even with apps like Instagram and FB's new filters, it is important to understand what you are doing to get the best picture. Sure, we can take thousands of pictures a year, but what if you want just one photograph *worth* saving. A good photo editing program can be the digital dark room that turns the common into the extraordinary. However, while it would be nice to offer programs on Adobe Photoshop and Lightroom, working the patrons up to this point takes a little more time and effort than this class does. Also, those programs offer more than what most people need. Whether or not you have a media program, you can teach this class and offer something that not only helps patrons understand how to make a great picture, but also what makes those pictures in *National Geographic* and the photography books shelved in the 700s worth examining.

WHAT PATRONS WILL NEED

- Basic computer skills
- An email account
- A camera phone, point-and-shoot digital camera, or single-lens reflex (SLR) camera
- An event they want to promote or host

WHAT YOU WILL NEED

- Some images with composition lines, and some images to edit
- Ability to display an active computer screen (projector monitor or enough room for everyone to gather around)
- An open Internet connection
- A PhotoCat account
- Access to an email account
- An SD card reader (not always necessary)

OUTLINE

1. Explain the basics of composition
2. Show patrons how to download or transfer images
   a. DCIM folders
3. Open images in PhotoCat and edit them
   a. Cropping and resizing
   b. Color
4. Upload photos for social media or save to the cloud

THE BIG PICTURE

Even though everyone is taking pictures with camera phones, the tricky part for many is removing them from the camera or phone. This program is designed to be a quick class on how to make pictures look good and take them off the phone, and will cover some basics of composition. Obviously, this will not be as flashy as a class on filters, but it is made to appeal to people who actually want to save and keep photos. A good way to promote this is to explain how to make better images by understanding images. PhotoCat can be pretty powerful when compared to working on the basics or cropping with phone apps. Sometimes a picture needs to be zoomed in larger than what our fingers can spread.

CLASS

Explain the Basics of Composition

The easiest way to get a good photo from editing is to take a good photo. A good photo comes from good composition. Good composition can be taught on any platform, but you don't need a computer to use it. When you go over these basic concepts, explain to the patrons that there is a way of seeing when taking pictures. What goes into the frame makes the picture. They should look at photos in magazines and on television, and maybe even look at some of the art books to see that understanding some elements, and how they are used, are how good images are made. Although a lot of good photo examples were taken in the traditional format, it doesn't really matter. A smartphone defaults to vertical, but we can simply turn the phone on its side. It doesn't matter if the patron uses horizontal or vertical (or landscape versus portrait) for composition. Think of what you want to get in the frame, and use the phone appropriately.

Rule of Thirds

Images should always have some sort of symmetry. People like an image with symmetry; the human mind just finds it comfortable. The most basic rule of thumb for shooting photos is the rule of threes. Break a frame into a grid with nine sections, and the focal point will always somehow center on one of those lines. You can find many examples online, and should walk the patrons through some famous images that use this rule. Even a portrait that is centered will almost always have the eyes sit one-third of the way down the image. So even when something is right in the middle of an image, it is still using the rule of thirds. This is more obvious, though, to the patron if you use an asymmetric composition like the image below.

> **PRO TIP**
>
> **Show a simple sample image that conforms to the rule of thirds, and then crop it so it does not, such as a head shot where the eye line is in the wrong space. Show both images to the patrons and ask them which is better. Then show them again with a grid like the one shown in the image below.**

> **PRO TIP**
>
> **This class is a good way to promote books on photography in your library collection. Hand out some books after going over these rules, and ask the patrons to find an example that displays one of these concepts. Then have them share their example with others in the class. Remember to tell them that they can check out these books after class.**

Negative Space

Negative space in an image helps not only balance, but also calls attention to the subject of the image. The idea of negative space is that there is less to distract from what you want to be the center of attention. Sometimes removing things that distract from the center of attention, basically creating negative space, can save an im-

The rule of thirds helps create balance in an image. ***https://commons.wikimedia.org/wiki/User:Chaky***

Cropping can help isolate action and remove distractions in an image. ***Courtesy Tim Green. http://timgreenfromqueensbury.blogspot.com/***

age. The images on page XX provide an example from WikiMedia, where cropping *increased* negative space.

An image is sometimes better if it has an element that gives it a sense of depth. This is usually achieved by setting the lens a certain way so that items in the background are out of focus. Camera phones are generally bad at this. Another trick is to have foreground interest, usually used in landscape; a foreground element gives the viewer a sense of the space. Look at the photograph below; notice that it has a fence in the foreground, which provides a sense of how large the mountains are.

Foreground items to show depth and give a sense of space

If patrons ask why they are learning this, explain that when an image is not well composed, that is when we must use the editing tools. The first step is getting the image off the phone.

Show Patrons How to Download or Transfer Images

For a smartphone, have the patrons email the images to their accounts through the interface. Apple and Android will do this. While a cable can be used for this as well, these sometimes have problems recognizing a phone or getting permission from the phone to access its files. You can do this on iPhones and androids from the mail functions. For a point-and-shoot or SLR camera, you can connect these directly to a computer with a USB cable. The computer will recognize the camera as an external drive. You can also use an SD card reader. The benefit of using a card reader is that during the class, you don't have to deal with plugging the phone into the computer. In case the patrons ask, the benefit to shooting with an SD card is that the photographer can replace the card in the camera with a fresh one when the camera memory has run out of space. The patron can download the images later without having to use the camera. It is surprising how many people only ever use one card in their camera.

DCIM FOLDERS When you open your Explorer or Finder window, and select the camera or SD card, you will see a DCIM folder. If you connect a smartphone to the camera, you will also find a DCIM folder. I have never encountered a device that did not keep images in a DCIM folder. This is a great tip for your patrons. Many times, if you hook a smartphone to a computer via USB, you can download images from the DCIM folder without loading iTunes or Android File Transfer. And if you don't know which drive is the camera or SD card (since this could be either drive I or drive J, depending on the computer), the easiest way to find your card or camera is to open drives until you find the DCIM folder.

Once the DCIM folder is located, patrons should leave this open in the browser while they open PhotoCat.

Open Files in PhotoCat and Edit

Explain to your patrons that PhotoCat is an online picture editor, and that there are several out there "in the wild," as we say. What that means is you can find other editors on the web. PhotoCat is the one we will use because, while it must be installed, it can be installed in the browser of any PC as an application. (It can also be downloaded as an app, and used from Facebook.)

Other reasons PhotoCat is one of the better photo editors include:

- It is free
- It uses some of the same icons and language as more advanced editors like Photoshop
- Unlike app editors on a phone, it has more customization
- It is cloud based, so once you have uploaded an image and added it to your Gallery, the image can be edited directly from your browser, or any browser from which you log into your account.

There is a caveat about using PhotoCat. Unlike some apps, if you apply filters and effects in PhotoCat, you must also save them. Sometimes people are confused because the filter is shown and they log out, only to later find that the new image was not saved. When you apply a filter, this creates a temporary image for you to look at, and you can undo this at any point. The changes are not permanent until you save them.

Now you can go over the actual functions in PhotoCat and actually let the patrons do the editing.

CROPPING AND RESIZING When you open PhotoCat, the interface defaults to a menu with effects, frame, stickers, and other items that we want to bypass for now. Look at the menu; there are two arrows at either end. Click on the arrow on the right, after the icon

The basic photo editing elements in PhotoCat

for orientation, so the menu looks like the image on the next page.

You will see that cropping is the first option on the new menu. Tell the patrons once again that we start with cropping because it changes composition, and composition is the *main* way to make a good image. That talk at the beginning of the class is important because we now know when to crop and why.

PRO TIP

Give the patrons an image to start the class, either preloaded or have them grab the same image from the web. Find something with a very definite object of interest, but small enough in frame so that it can be recomposed multiple ways. Ask your patrons to reframe it using the rule of threes, and then have them show their result to each other. Most of the time they will have different compositions.

There should be *some* difference in how they used the framing, so point out that, even though it is a "rule," how it is applied leaves a lot of artistic freedom.

Load a photograph onto the screen; it is best if the image has something with a very obvious center of interest, like a flower or a person. If you click on the crop icon, this menu will open. PhotoCat displays a nice grid that complies with the rule of thirds. First show your patrons how to crop:

- Reframe the image so that the item in the image conforms to the rule of thirds. The area inside the grid is your selection, and the grayed-out area will be cropped out.
- On the right is the Apply button; click it. The image is replaced in the interface with just your selection.

PhotoCat's interface will allow a crop to be made freestyle or according to a certain aspect ratio. Click and hold on a circle in the corner, which will allow you to drag and resize the frame around the picture. You can also click and hold inside the image to move the picture around inside the frame.

It is a good idea to talk a little about aspect ratios. These are important for printed images if patrons would like to put the images in videos or want to be consistent across images. Most commercial photo printing is done at a 3:2 ratio; the table is a diagram of the aspect ratios for common print sizes.

Aspect ratio	3:2	4:3	5:4
Size in inches of common photo print options	4×6 6×9 8×12 10×15	9×12 12×16 15×20 18×24	4×5 8×10 16×20 24×30

The best use of the resize image is to make sure that the image is large enough to print. Images from modern cell phones and point-and-shoot cameras almost *always* are large enough. Beyond this, resizing will be a little more difficult to explain to patrons. Size in pixels, which is how an image is measured, is different from size in inches, which is its output. For the most part this is important only for printing, where pixels per inch (PPI) or dots per inch (DPI) are used for different types of printing. However, this can cause confusion because a video or computer monitor will ignore this restriction for the most part. A TV screen, a printer, and a photo image can all have the same aspect ratio, have the same number of pixels, and display at different sizes.

The resolutions of different media are:

- Video or computer monitor: usually 72 to 196 PPI
- Print text or newspaper: 150 PPI
- Print text or book: 300 PPI
- Print photograph: 1200 PPI

Think of pixels as colored balls. A computer screen uses golf balls, a printout marbles, and photo, ball bearings. So a 1-inch by 1-inch box holds fewer golf balls than marbles or ball bearings. Yet they are all round and come in the same colors, so they can be used to make the same picture. For the last several years we have had the idea that larger images and more megapixels, is a better image, and while that is true, it is not important if there are more pixels than a monitor can display. So when you talk about size in pixels:

- It is *most* important to print
- It is important if you have a very *large* image and would like to make it smaller for video or web
- Do not change the number, unless you are sure what the output is (print, video, or web).

Lighting and Color

The next two icons are lighting and color. These concepts will be hard to explain, but easy to show. Com-

Lighting and Color options interface

pared to more robust programs like Photoshop, the controls are very basic. However, these are basic concepts that run across many programs.

The slider is your only tool. Slide toward positive and the editor adds brightness; sliding toward negative makes it darker. The different tabs do the following:

- Brightness will raise the overall white in an image
- Contrast will push dark colors darker and light colors lighter
- Highlights will affect only the lighter areas
- Shadows affect only the darker areas

The Color options are a little more difficult to explain, but are easy to show. Click on the color options, then show your patrons.

> **PRO TIP**
>
> **A good idea is to have either the image of the color wheel or an actual color wheel available when explaining the Tint process. Many color wheels can be found online, but a physical one that can be passed around will give the patrons a chance to stop staring at their screen.**

- Saturation will add more color. In general, it makes the picture "brighter" or makes it "pop" (good for photos on overcast days).
- Warmth will make the whole image more red or blue (good for photos taken outside in direct light or under incandescent bulbs).
- Tint is very similar, except that it changes the color over a wider range, so blue can become green can become purple. Tint will shift the colors.
- Fade washes an image out, or removes color and brightness from the image; it is very similar to contrast and lightness combined with saturation, but doesn't raise the level of white in the image. (It can be used to call attention to a specific item by making it more colorful, so that it is more dominant in the image.)

When explaining these options, make sure that you show them as well. If a patron asks why there is a face control when you could use brightness and saturation and lightness, I do not have an answer.

> **PRO TIP**
>
> **I am not a big fan of filters in general; they are quickly overused for images and lose their impact. Like the basics of composition, it might be worthwhile to let the patrons play with the color correction and focus tools to try and recreate the filters, so they understand how the effect is made. It will also show them that more than one filter or color correction can be combined to create new and interesting effects.**

FOCUS, FILTERS, AND ENHANCE PhotoCat has more options besides Cropping and Resizing, Brightness and Color adjustments. Three others I will talk about are Focus, Filters, and Enhance. I bring these up because they offer a lot of "bang for the buck" in a presentation. They can easily make a good image look better, but are more likely used to make a mediocre image look mediocre in a completely different way. Discussing these is a good way to finish up a presentation on photo editing. The patrons or you can explore them at leisure.

Focus should actually be named blur, since it blurs part of the image. This option will select an area, a circle or square, and keeps it in focus while blurring the rest of the image. Demonstrating focus is a good time to revisit depth of field, since this is what it is emulating.

Everything has filters now. Originally Photoshop was the only way to provide this function, but Instagram has spread cheap and easy-to-use effects. You can play with these at your leisure, but generally these do several color and brightness corrections to an image at once to recapture a vintage or other specific feel.

The Enhancements options are also basically filters; however, they are more geared toward the content of an image than the "feel" of the final product, and include Hi-Def, Scenery, Food, Portrait, and Night. These work well on the subject matter they were designed to enhance, but they can also be used like filters to create more interesting images.

How to Load up on Social Media Download or Save to the Cloud

PhotoCat is made to save images to Facebook. By having used the online version of PhotoCat, you have saved your work on the PhotoCat server. By default, it is "in the cloud" already. However, if you want others to see your image, it will have to be shared, and sometimes that means bringing it to a local computer. There is a Share on FB button available in the main toolbar. On the splash page, however, if you do not want to simply share your photo on FB and would rather download or send it directly, there is that option. Clicking it will bring up the Download menu, as shown below.

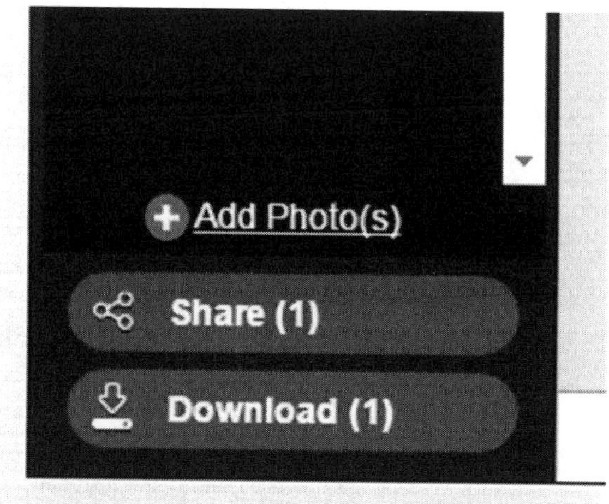

PhotoCat includes Social and Download options.

Two things will happen with this interface that could cause confusion. One is the fact that the URL provided is only useful while this image is in your cloud. The second is that when you download, it defaults to a compressed ZIP file, so you will need to explain that a ZIP file may need to be opened with the appropriate software. It is not usually a problem with Windows machines, but it could be if your patrons are using older machines, or non-Windows machines.

> **PRO TIP**
>
> **Ask your patrons to share their retouched photos on FB, and ask them to tag the location as your library or mention the class there. It is a great way to grow awareness of your library's programs and social media presence.**

HOW THE TOPIC CAME UP AND BECAME A CLASS

A lovely patron needed me to explain how to download her images from a camera and send via email at least once every three weeks. To make the pictures fit within her email file size limitations, I would have to open up an image editing program to make the pictures smaller. Then about every time we transferred her photos off the camera, I would end up helping her tweak them a little for a better image. The fact that some of these pictures were of her watercolors made the process a little harder. She loved to push the saturation, making them more colorful than they really were. We never actually decided on how ethical that process was.

She was wonderful and lost, and I was looking for an easy way for her to share her images and not have to move them into a completely different program. All the resources that went into working with her became this class. When she asked me to help some of her friends who were painters as well, it became a very specific class for her friends. However, I realized a lot of the "techy" stuff, as she called it, was basic to all image sharing.

Your YouTube Channel

How to Set up a Channel for Your Home Videos and Keep Them Private, or Not

WHY BOTHER?

There are several ways to share videos online. YouTube has been the number one way to do it for years. Taking videos may be easy, but uploading and sharing them takes a little skill. Compared to using Facebook or other social media sites to share directly, YouTube has much better privacy and editing, and touches on more media literacy. When I was running this program, FB did not handle video.

WHAT PATRONS WILL NEED

- Basic computer skills
- A Gmail account or YouTube account
- Videos to share

WHAT YOU WILL NEED

- A Gmail account or YouTube account
- Ability to display an active computer screen (projector monitor or enough room for everyone to gather around)
- An open Internet connection
- Speakers connected to your computer

OUTLINE

1. Setting Up an Account
   a. If patrons do not have a Gmail account, make one
   b. Show how YouTube is connected to Google
2. Loading a Video
   a. How to load up a video through YouTube
   b. Privacy settings
3. Review YouTube editing functions
   a. Creator Studio
   b. Creating a playlist
   c. Enhancing or not
   d. Sharing with people and getting subscribers

THE BIG PICTURE

This class shows patrons how to set up a YouTube channel for home videos and explains privacy settings. It explains the best way to load content, share with others, and make videos available to others.

CLASS

When you start teaching patrons how to upload YouTube videos, your first question will be, do they have videos? However, this actually depends on whether a patron has a Google account. If the patron has one, great, it will make life easier. If not, then you need to set up an account. I am sure your library has run a program on making email accounts, but I will gloss over the steps for you.

Setting up a Google Account

First make sure that your patrons can receive text notifications. This will be important. Now open Gmail. When the patron is on the login screen, he or she can use any name. It is *important* to stress, however, that he or she will *not* need to disclose this email when using Google Voice. It is possible to use a private email just as it is possible to use a private phone for Google Voice. If, however, your patrons do not have a "professional email" account, it is a good idea to kill two birds with one stone.

The login screen will ask for a name. It only accepts A–Z, 1–0 and a period (.) as entries. Be careful not to get tied up in this step; way too often when creating names for email accounts, the preferred name is taken. Just add a period, followed by phone (.phone) to any name they come up with, and a number after that if necessary. It can take a long time to find something unused if users are trying to get creative.

Next, Gmail will want the name, birthday, and sex of the user. Try and encourage patrons to use real information, as it can be important if they start using this account beyond the phone. Then Gmail will ask for a cell phone number. It is important that patrons

> **PRO TIP**
>
> **Google accounts have many functions. One of the more annoying functions is the fact that the Google Chrome browser links to the user. You may need to clear the browser before or after classes.**

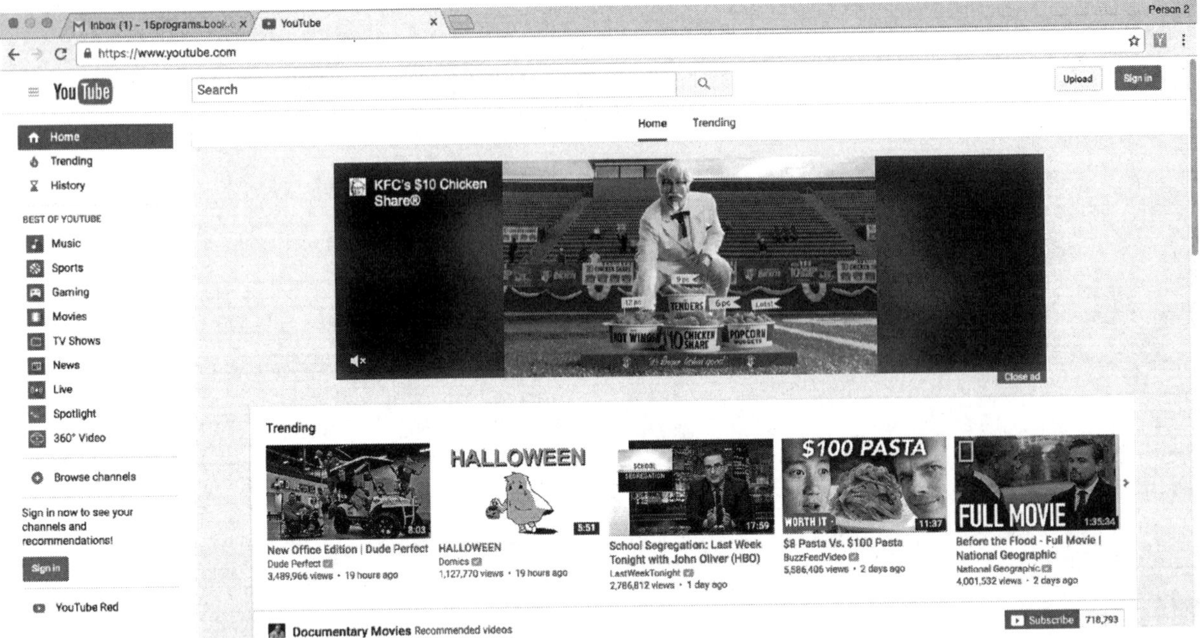

YouTube main interface, the first step in creating an account

provide a correct phone number. When they try to use the account, Google will use text notifications to activate and check the account.

To see how YouTube is connected, tell your patrons to *not* log out of their Gmail account. Simply navigate to YouTube. When the site loads, you will see a screen like the one shown above.

In the upper-right corner you should be able to sign in and upload. After you have signed in, you will be asked to create a channel. Creating a channel is important, because you can allow others to share that channel. You can later connect other accounts to the channel, including other people's accounts. Once the channel is created, you can load videos.

PRO TIP

Patrons may have a very hard time loading videos; they may be indecisive or unwilling to share the video. Have some video clips ready for them, either preloaded to the computer, or on a thumb drive. It is also a good idea to have two or more videos to work with.

Loading a Video

The load process is very simple, easier in fact than transferring files from a thumb drive. It does, however, require that the patrons provide videos and know how to transfer them from a thumb drive (or you will need to provide one).

When you click on the icon to upload a video, it will bring up the interface shown in the figure below. First you can choose one of the three options: Public, Unlisted, or Private. For now, have your patrons choose Private; this can be changed later. Simply clicking on the arrow in the box will open a file browser. Select your video, and it will start loading.

Once the video loads, YouTube will bring you to a new interface. We can now talk more about the privacy settings.

Select files to upload

Or drag and drop video files

The Upload interface is drag-and-drop, with an option to control who can find it.

The patrons have selected Private (remember, the other two options are Public and Unlisted). Public will, as the name suggests, allow your videos to be accessed by anyone on YouTube, so one reason to avoid this is privacy concerns. You will notice that to the right of the video interface is the Privacy option once again. This interface can be opened from the YouTube video manager.

At this point, your patrons should have an account and a loaded video. It may take longer for some videos to load than others, so this is a good break point for your class. A good thing to do at this point is ask the patrons what kind of videos they would like to share, who they would like to share with, and how they obtain their videos. If a patron has a 15-minute video, it could take an hour to process and YouTube will be compressing it for playback. Please advise patrons to choose shorter videos.

Review YouTube Editing Functions

The majority of your editing functions in YouTube are available from the Creator Studio. Some of these functions are available on the load screen, and it makes sense to do these during the load. However, you want to make sure patrons can access this screen for the next step, so it is better to enter the Creator Studio.

CREATOR STUDIO If you click on Account in the upper-right corner, an interface will open for Creator Studio. Creator Studio is where you can make edits, manage, and monetize a YouTube channel. We will only be concerned with two of the three items on the menu that comes up on the left: Dashboard, Video Manager, and Create.

CREATING A PLAYLIST If you select Video Manager, this will open two options, Video and Playlist. By choosing Edit on the Video, you can open it back up to Basic, and see the same options as when you were loading your video. Tags and descriptions are not

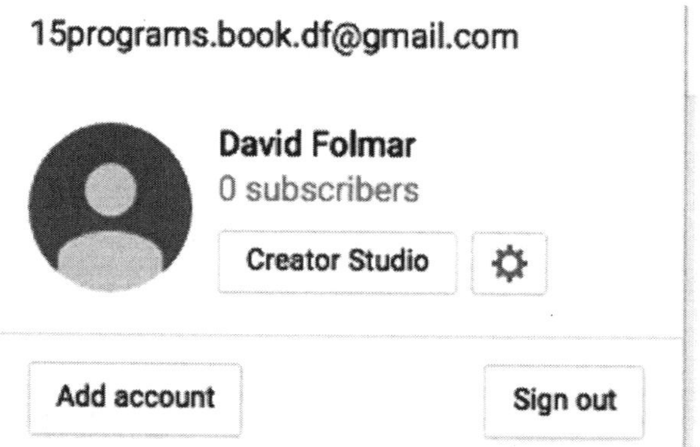

The Creator Studio button is easy to miss, but important.

PRO TIP

You might set up a YouTube channel for your library, and send patrons attending the class a link to it. Ask them to share their videos, and brand this as a community video page for the class.

necessary because we are privately sharing directly with people. Translations and Advanced Settings can also be ignored. However, here is where you can change the privacy settings, or add the video to an existing playlist. You will also notice that a video can be shared here. Since we do not have a playlist, you would need to create one using the Playlist option under Video Manager.

Why would we creating a playlist? Well, we are assuming that people will have more than one video to share. Playlists will let us combine videos, add to them, and otherwise change them *without* having to share them again. Others with access to your Channel can also add to a playlist. So, for example, you could have multiple people adding videos to a family reunion event.

Have your patrons click Playlists. Select New Playlist from the upper-right corner. They will again select a Privacy setting, but this will not be the same as the video setting! If you want to make this playlist searchable, the figures on page 22 show where you can do this under the Playlist settings.

The Basic setting is where you can control the Privacy, and Collaborate is where you can invite others to add video. Patrons can send collaborators a link to add video to an event. Once they have created a playlist, it is then just a matter of adding videos to it and sharing. Click Add Videos on the right-hand side of the playlist description. It will call up the interface shown on page 23.

If you click on Your YouTube Videos, you can select the videos the patrons have loaded and add them in turn. The option of the Video Search will also allow this to be used to share interesting videos from other sources with people. So this can be used not just for families, but for interest groups too, say to share videos about a civic cause or a sports team. Once you have added the videos, there is again the option to Share. We will hold off on that for now.

TO ENHANCE OR NOT ENHANCE YouTube gives users an option for enhancing video. If you go back to the Video Manager, and click Edit next to the video title, you will have options for making enhancements to

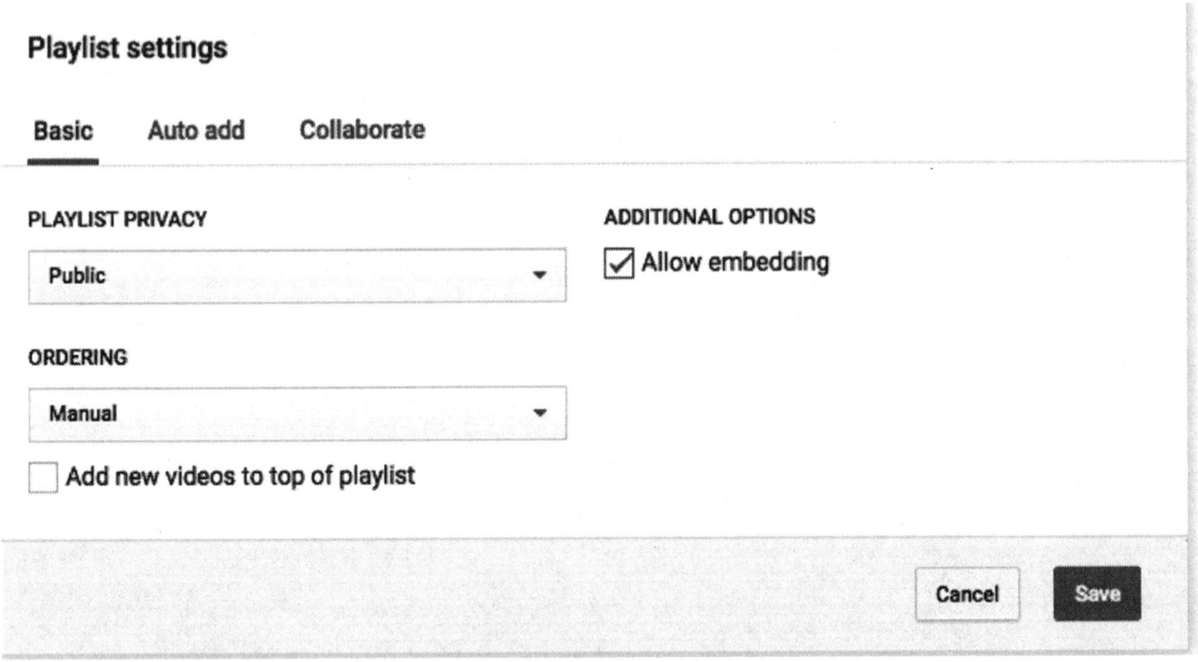

Playlist privacy and embedding will allow video to be shared, with some control.

the video. This does an okay job; it is not always terrible. In general, it is not great either. I have not been pleased with the results, especially on longer clips. The YouTube Audio and End Titles are more useful.

Audio is not much appreciated by people until it is missing. Go back to the dashboard, choose Create, then select Audio Library. This will give some royalty-free music to choose from, which can be downloaded and added to a video. You can then save your video as a new video. You can similarly add end screens, or text and graphics following the video. A video must be 25 seconds long for this. Patrons can also use the YouTube Video Editor to add titles and text to a video. Like music, after these are added, the video can be saved as a new video, which is what we want to do.

Sharing with People and Getting Subscribers

At this point your patrons will want to share their playlists, *not* the videos. Sharing the playlist will allow users to make changes to its content, and allow others to add to it without having to reshare. Open up Playlists under the Video Manager. If your patrons have added music to a video, have them save this, and delete the original video. Videos can be deleted by

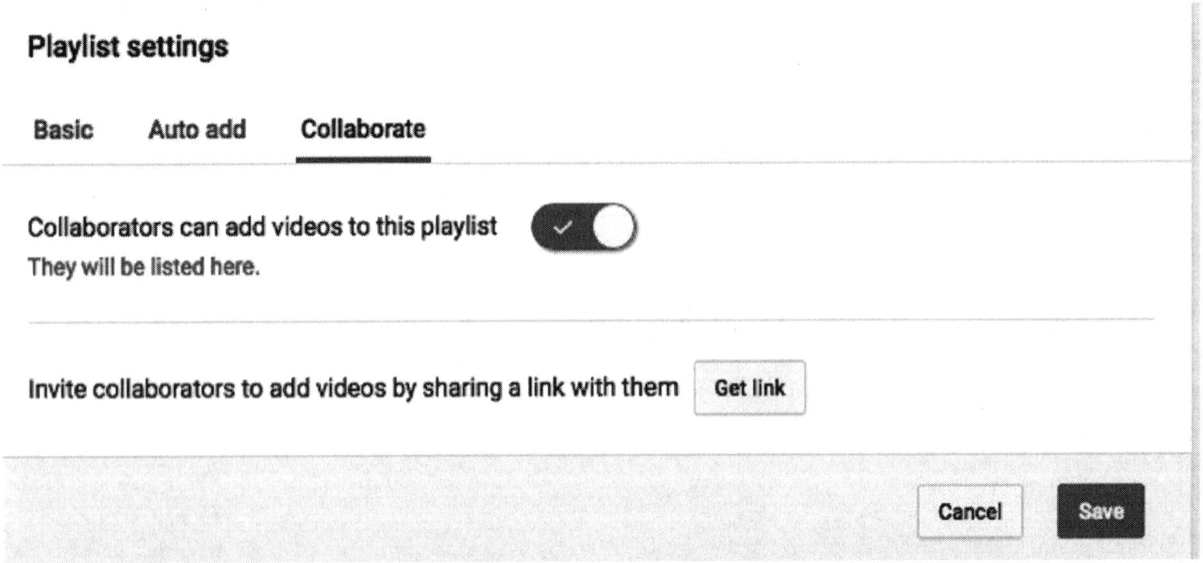

Allowing collaborators can make a YouTube playlist or account accessible to family and friends.

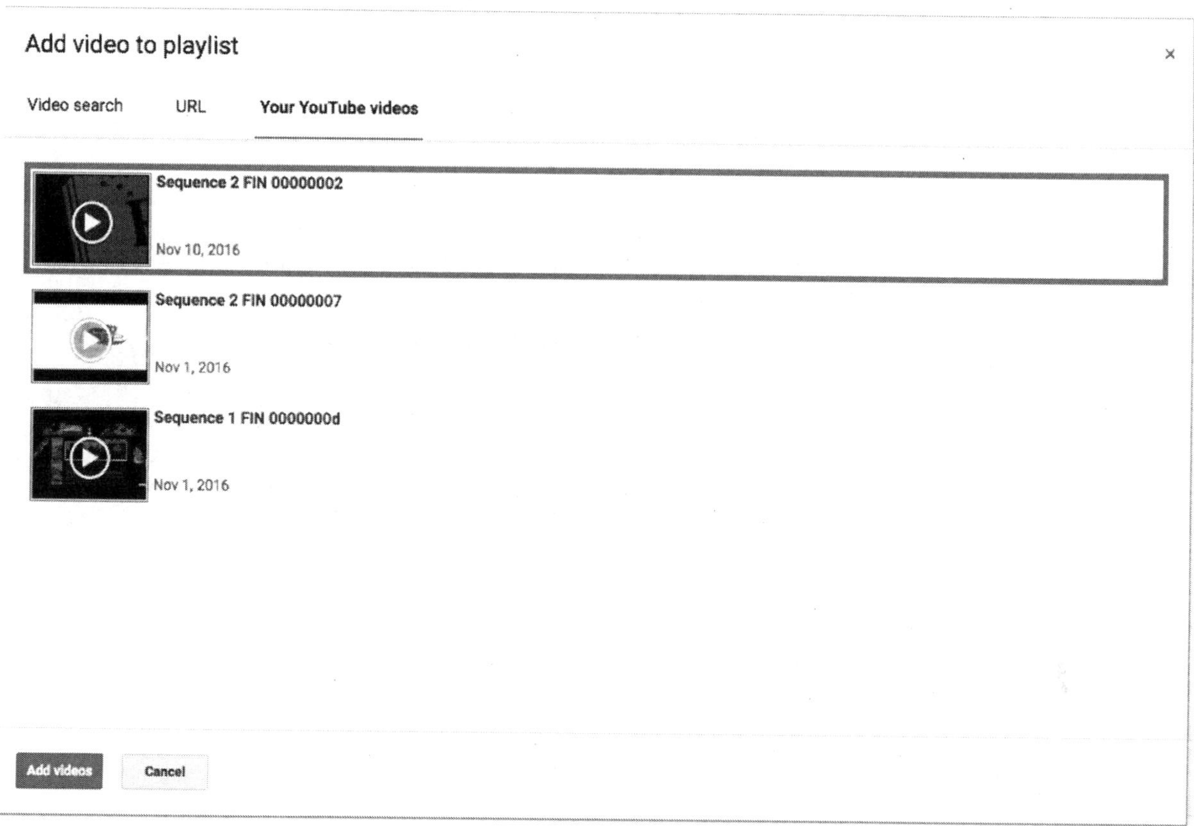

A playlist can be used to share a number of videos from different sources.

mousing over the video in the list; click on it, and an X will pop up in the corner. Click the X to delete. Now your patrons will know how to edit and refine their playlist. Finally, they can share it. Click on Share and you will see a new interface, shown below.

If your patrons do not know how to share the playlist, show them how to add this to FB, or email the link. Call attention to the fact that this allows people with the link to add videos. If you share this on FB, anyone they share this with will be able to add to the playlist. Do *not* click on this unless patrons do not mind losing the ability to control the playlist. If they do want to allow others to add to the playlist, use the collaborators function.

HOW THE TOPIC CAME UP AND BECAME A CLASS

A patron named Teddy inspired this class. She is a person of strong civic and community convictions, who had a huge amount of video. In trying to help her share and maintain her collection, I saw an opportunity. Having video production experience meant that I was the de facto resource for anything having to do

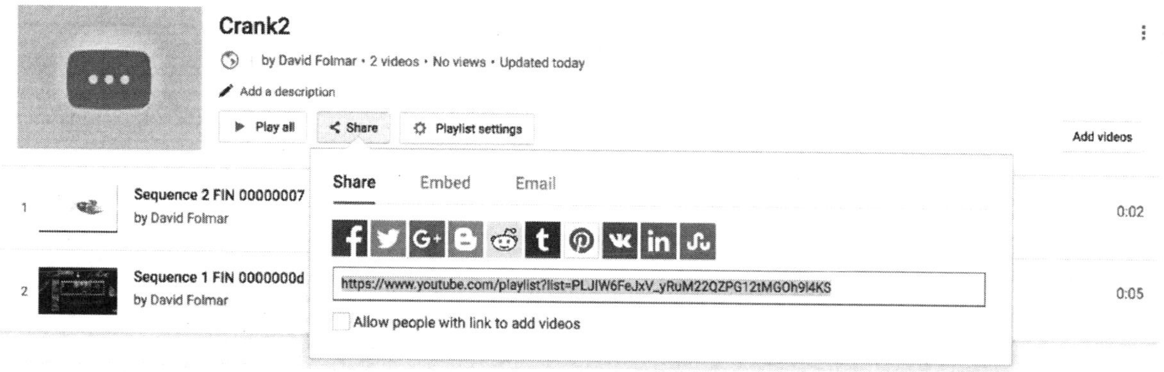

An option allows those people you share your playlist with to contribute their own videos.

with video. In Teddy's case, it was obvious that simply transferring from VHS or her phone to a CD or DVD was not realistic.

Her need to share and collaborate, and maintain control over and keep separate her private life, made me realize that YouTube could be used in different ways to help people. The playlist function and allowing others to use it go beyond simple sharing; it can be used collaboratively for a PTA, community sports teams, civic groups or, as the class is built around, family life. My experiences teaching this are that people often have video that they are not sure how to keep or to share. At the time I developed this class, FB did not allow video to be uploaded, so this was the best solution.

Even with FB allowing video, YouTube still features some unique controls and abilities, like the editing and adding audio functions as well as the ability to create "private" online resources that your patrons may find useful.

Redecorate in 3D—Don't Break Your Back

Sweet Home 3D for Renovating or Redesigning Your Home

WHY BOTHER?

Using computer programs to address real-world problems is the idea behind these classes. I can't think of a bigger problem than trying to decide how to rearrange a room or buy a new piece of furniture. Well, to be fair, the problem is usually disagreement between spouses or roommates on whether the changes will really work. One person wants a new chair; the other person doesn't think it will fit (or at least, that is the excuse for not liking the La-Z-Boy recliner). One could get out the measuring tape and try and convince the other into imagining it, but why not put the measurements to a better use? With a program like Sweet Home 3D, your patrons can create virtual rooms and try out several configurations. At one time this would have been impossible for a homeowner, but now it is fairly simple. The fun part with a program like this is that you are teaching not only the basics about layout and spatial relationships, but also underlying ideas about three-dimensional creation, and computer simulation as a time- and money-saving device.

WHAT PATRONS WILL NEED

- Basic computer skills
- A tape measure (don't need to bring it)

WHAT YOU WILL NEED

- A copy of Sweet Home 3D for your computers or lab computers
- Ability to display an active computer screen (projector monitor or enough room for everyone to gather around)
- A thumb drive, or have patrons bring their own computers
- An open Internet connection
- Measurements for the room in which you are giving the class

OUTLINE

1. Finding, loading, and opening Sweet Home 3D
   a. The Sweet Home 3D interface
2. Measuring and creating a room
   a. Measuring a room and creating a room based on those measurements
   b. Building walls, windows, and doors
   c. Customizing rooms
3. Installing furniture
   a. Choosing furniture
   b. Modifying furniture
4. Moving around furniture and saving configurations
   a. Viewing your room
   b. Saving different versions

THE BIG PICTURE

You will be walking patrons through creating a room and putting furniture in it using Sweet Home 3D. In some classes, it might be necessary to walk them through actually using a measuring tape or laser distance measure. Remember, not all STEM skills are on a computer.

The class works best when the software is preloaded and existing room models are provided. My suggestion is to walk them through the interface using a model of the room you are teaching in. Create models of the room and of furniture ahead of time. As you walk through these steps, you can have measurements ready, and if you encounter a problem or a sticking point, you can provide the appropriate model to your patrons.

CLASS

Finding, Loading, and Opening Sweet Home 3D

Sweet Home 3D is free software and can be found at http://www.sweethome3d.com. It is a site maintained by the owners, and could also be used on that site as an app if you prefer not to download it. It is worth the effort to download, but for instructional purposes, you can simply use the online version. The site also contains free 3D models as well as the software. These are not especially useful for this class that focuses on layout, but mention it to the patrons. They may find playing with different models to be fun. The new models are also useful if users wish to explore some of the visualization and image creation tools.

One of the benefits of this software is that it is platform independent, and runs on Windows, Mac, and

PRO TIP

The Sweet Home 3D website is in Dutch, so to view it for download, use Google Chrome to translate the site to English. Also, the download is through SourceForge servers. It might be a good idea to download this to a thumb drive in advance to hand out.

Linux. The program is built in Java, so it will work on any computer that runs a modern browser such as Chrome or Firefox. Also important to note is that the download will direct through SourceForge; do not be confused when the site redirects you.

The Sweet Home 3D Interface

Now you can open Sweet Home. The basic layout looks like the figure below.

- Toolbar across the top
- Left top pane is the library of items, or furniture catalog
- Right top pane is the design area, or Home Plan
- Below that is the Home 3D View
- The remaining area is furniture and additional items

Across the top of the screen is the toolbar. The toolbar is composed of four sections; you will need the first three for this class. They are:

- File functions
  - New, Open, Save, Undo, Redo, Cut, Copy, Paste
  - Add Furniture
- Plan tools for room navigation and creation, and text controls. The important ones in this section are:
  - Selection tool
  - Grab or Move tools
  - Create Walls
  - Create Room
  - Create Dimensions (useful for making hallways that comply with the Americans with Disabilities Act, or setting aside space for traffic flow)

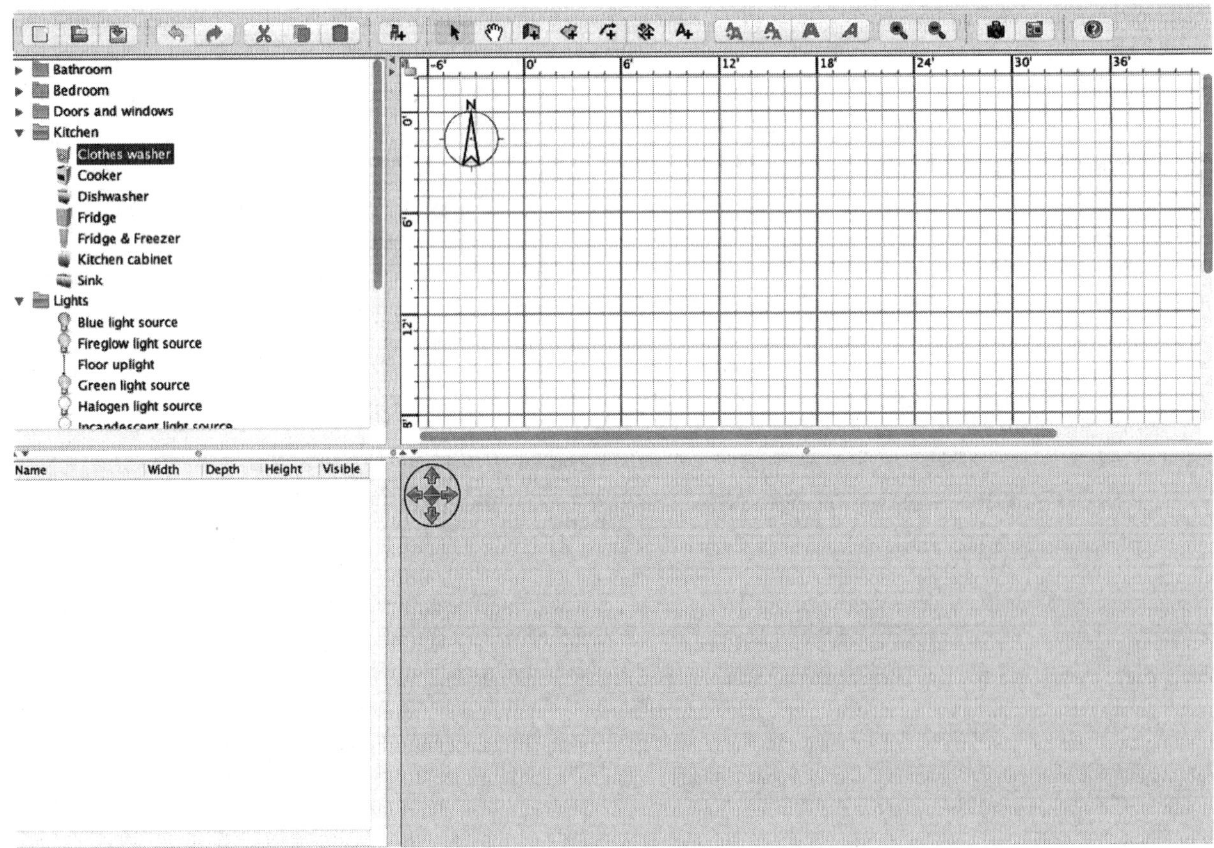

The main Sweet Home 3D interface

A pop-up explains what each icon does when you mouse over it.

MEASURING AND CREATING A ROOM The room will only be helpful if it actually reflects the room the patrons have at home, so they must measure their room. It is beyond the scope of the class to measure their rooms, but it might be helpful to go over some of the basics with patrons:

- Rooms are measured on an X/Y scale, X being width and Y, length
- When dealing with a 3D model, dimensions will be width × depth × height
- 1 foot equals 12 inches
- The foot abbreviation is ' and the inch abbreviation is "
- always make your measurements as exact as possible

PRO TIP

Have the patrons measure the room you are teaching in. It is a good way for them to move around and interact. Break them into teams and get measurements for walls, desks or tables, and other items. Bring a laser distance measure to the class and show them how easy it is to use. Most contractors use one, but some homeowners may have never used one. They are much simpler to use than tape measures.

- First, have the patrons click on Create Room.
- Click in the grid (the 0 spot on the graph is advisable) then move the mouse across until the small box reads the width of the room; click again, then drag the mouse down until you get the length in the box.
- You should now have a triangle. If you move the cursor back toward your starting point, you can create a square. When the room is the shape you want, double-click inside the room you have drawn, or click off the grid.
- You can also create irregular shaped rooms by adding more points to a side. Play with it to see this.

Again, it is advisable to premeasure a room for your patrons. Put those measurements up separately as you walk through them. I would suggest not using the 3D interface to display these; instead, use PowerPoint or similar software, and then display the room after the patrons have made an attempt.

BUILDING WALLS, WINDOWS, AND DOORS Once you have the general outline of the room, you can add walls. The Build Walls icon is located after the Move icon and before the Create Room icon. Remember, mousing over the icons displays their names. The process is identical to building rooms:

1. Click the icon
2. Clik a corner and hold
3. Drag, and a wall will display as you do
4. Double-click to end

The major difference is that this does not auto-fill the shape, in other words, if the wall runs all the way around a room, it will not add a wall to complete a shape. However, if you look at the box below the grid, you will see that a 3D object is created. The walls will have a height, whereas the room did not. The patrons should have an empty room in which to place doors and windows.

There is an option in the menu bar for adding furniture or doors. To use this, you must select an item from the menu on the left-hand side of the interface. However, it is usually easier to just use the Select tool. With Select, you can simply click on the item you want to add and drag it into the room.

The third option is the Door and Windows drop-down menu. Open it to find a variety of door and window styles. Windows and Doors can be placed directly *into* walls. By default, these should center inside the wall's depth. If they do not, you can correct this. On the toolbar is a Zoom In and Zoom Out tool. Zooming in will provide finer control over objects in the room, and you can center them that way. Display for your patrons the process of placing a door:

1. Click on the door and drag into a wall. It will auto-center in the depth of the wall.
2. Now double-click on the door in the Home Plan. This will open the Modify Furniture interface.

Now is a good time to show patrons the precreated room. Add color to your room beforehand, so that you you can segue into the next section more easily.

CUSTOMIZING ROOMS Your patrons' walls and room in the 3D space will be white at first. So how can they make the room look like the room displayed? The trick

The Modification interface can be used to customize objects, including walls.

to customizing rooms is color and textures. Click on the Select Object in Plan Tool; it is the arrow icon. Double-click on your wall, and the screen shown above will pop up.

You will notice that there are dimensions at the top of the interface that reflect the size of the room, and that the middle is divided into a left side and right side. Each side has options for color and texture. The textures provided in Sweet Home 3D are very realistic, but better ones can be downloaded.

White is the default color; if you click on Color, another pop-up offers you this palate pictured above. Click inside this box on the color desired, and click OK. The side of the wall is now the color. Double-click on the floor, and a similar interface opens; here you can use the textures. You should now have a room that is not just white.

INSTALLING FURNITURE This is another good time to talk with the patrons. Instead of having them choose a layout beforehand, ask them what they would like to see in this room. Start by asking them what kind of room it is. Try and get some sort of consensus about what kind of room it will be, and remember to make the room large enough to hold several pieces of furniture of various types.

Sweet Home 3D will allow custom colors and the creation of custom palates.

Once your patrons have decided on the kind of room they want, have them drag the appropriate furniture into the room. The process is identical to adding doors and windows, except that these will not be in the walls. You should choose the stick furniture from the menu on the left.

MODIFYING FURNITURE AND DOORS The doors and windows may not be the right size or height, or they may open in the wrong direction. The tables may not be the right size. Once patrons have one of each piece of furniture and the doors or windows in the room, we can start to modify them. We will again use the Select tool and double-click on the item we want to modify. The easiest modification you can make is moving the doors or furniture around. This is done simply by clicking on the selection tool and then clicking on and dragging the furniture. If you need to rotate a piece of furniture to set it at an angle, a Rotate option is located in the upper-right corner. Click on this and drag the piece to the appropriate angle.

Open a door or window interface, like the wall interface, by double-clicking on it with the Selection tool. You will see Location on the left and Size on the right. Look on the left at Location; the X and Y describe where on the grid this item is found. For most users, it is easier to drag the furniture around than use this interface. However, under these coordinates is the Elevation. For windows, this is useful for setting the height of the bottom of the window from the floor.

The Size option is more commonly used; the options are Width, Depth, and Height, and a check box for Mirrored Shape. Doors and windows usually come in a few common sizes and do not need modifying, but the mirrored shape is very important for doors. A door may need to open in the opposite

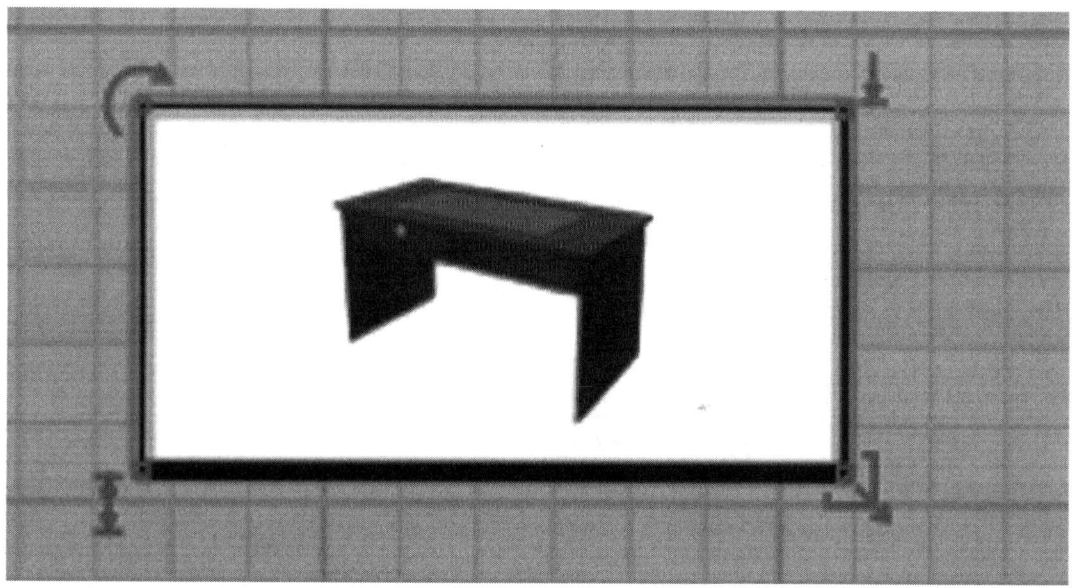

The size and position of objects can be modified in the main interface.

Name

Name: Door ☐ Display name in plan

Location

X (inch): 16'8⅜"

Y (inch): -0'0⅛"

Elevation (inch): 0'

Angle (°): 0

☑ Part of base plan

Size

Width (inch): 3'

Depth (inch): 0'9¾"

Height (inch): 6'10"

☐ Keep proportions

☑ Mirrored shape

Color and texture

○ Unchanged

○ Color:

◉ Texture:

○ Materials: Modify

Shininess

◉ Unchanged

○ Matt

○ Shiny

☑ Visible

Cancel OK

The Location part of the interface is important for fine-tuning positions and modifying the elevation of objects, like windows and doors.

> **PRO TIP**
>
> **You will also notice an angle box under Location; when you rotate furniture with the mouse, this number will change. It can be difficult to be very precise with the mouse in modifying rotation. While few (if any) people know the actual angle to the wall a piece of furniture sits, clicking in this box and adding a few degrees to the number can make rotation easier.**

direction, and checking Mirrored Shape will reverse the direction it opens.

Next you need to show patrons how to modify the furniture. It is basically the same process as for doors. You should go over measuring again, and talk about how to measure furniture. The trick with furniture is remembering that space needs to be kept between the wall and the furniture item. The size part of the interface is the Width and Height, so click on the numbers there and enter your measurements.

MOVING AROUND FURNITURE AND SAVING CONFIGURATIONS Once a room is completed, ask patrons if they can think of another layout, and let them try moving furniture. They should feel free to add or remove any furniture they choose. After 5 or 10 minutes, you can ask them to show each other what they have tried. Furniture moving is simple with the Selection tool (the arrow).

SAVING CONFIGURATIONS AND VIEWING ROOMS At this point, class members should be making a reasonable version of a room. Again, it does not need to look exact—only the dimensions are important. If, in the process of putting in furniture, a patron mistakenly clicks on a wall and affects it, remind them to use the Undo button. Also, if a patron somehow destroys a wall, I suggest having a version of the prebuilt room saved on the computer he or she is using. If patrons miss a window, or the wall is the wrong color, so be it. As long as they understand how to make walls and furniture, this is fine. Suggest to them that they try and think of a better layout for the room you have built. They can do whatever they want—add a couch, move desks, put in a window. Let them go to town; suggest they explore some of the furniture in the left-hand menu. See what will fit, and what will not. They can explore how this works to see what changing their own rooms will be like.

VIEW YOUR ROOM The final part of using Sweet Home 3D is the bottom-right viewing pane of the interface. It is the 3D part of the view. Clicking inside this pane will allow you to change the 3D view of the room. Click inside the pane, and hold the button.

- Left and Right will rotate the room
- Up and Down will change the angle of the view
- Scroll buttons zoom in and out.
- Generally, when working with 3D programs, this is the part of the process that takes the most time. One of the nice features of Sweet Home 3D is that the 3D view will not allow you to accidentally move items. Still, leave ample time for patrons to play. Tell them to look at the 3D view, zoom in and out, and consider changing the layout again based on how the 3D version looks.

SAVING DIFFERENT VERSIONS When patrons have changed the room to their liking, let them save it. On the top toolbar, to the right, is the Save button.

Like any file, different versions can be saved with slightly different names. Have patrons save this with their name; you should have a thumb drive or other media to save to, or another way to display their efforts. The beauty of this program is that they can open more than one room and compare how they look with the 3D view. So saving alternate versions is a best practice.

HOW THE TOPIC CAME UP AND BECAME A CLASS

This class was created because I had used Sweet Home 3D, and I was trying to teach a group of kids how to do some basic 3D work. They were using a slightly more advanced program, and one young girl was having a problem grasping the ideas behind 3D and controlling overlap. For the next time we were in the computer lab, I built a copy of the room and asked the kids to create a better layout. They enjoyed it quite a bit, and one of the children asked if she could have the program to redesign her own room, because her parents did not want her to. It seemed to me that along with creating an easy introduction to 3D programs, the class could have a real-life function too.

Crowdfund Me!

GoFundMe, CrowdRise, and Kickstarter

WHY BOTHER?

Crowdfunding is something that I feel should have been started by libraries. The tough economic reality is that sometimes, the money to make a better life is *not* there, and a great cause or idea will never be realized. In response, people have started crowdfunding sites as a way to directly interact with others to raise funds. There is a range of websites for crowdfunding. We will cover the top three, along with crowdfunding best practices. The goal of this class is to show the patrons crowdfunding sites, explain what needs to be done to use them, and provide them with best practices.

WHAT PATRONS WILL NEED

- Nothing except an idea

WHAT YOU WILL NEED

- Ability to display an active computer screen (projector monitor or enough room for everyone to gather around)
- An open Internet connection

OUTLINE

1. Crowdfunding: what is it?
   a. Which site is best for you?
2. GoFundMe
   a. What does it raise money for?
   b. What will it take to use the site?
   c. What will it take to make fundraising successful?
3. CrowdRise
4. Kickstarter
   a. What does it raise money for?
   b. What will it take to use the site?
   c. What will it take to make fundraising successful?
5. Other Crowdfunding sites to consider:
   a. RocketHub
   b. StartSomeGood
   c. Patreon

THE BIG PICTURE

Every interface is different, and every site caters to a slightly different audience. Much of making a successful crowdfunding site requires outside work, a video or images, social connections, or a good story, which really means that the bulk of the work takes place before you even log on. So rather than try to explain *how* to use a site, we are covering which site is best for a project, so that an app designer doesn't try to use Indiegogo or another site that is not optimal for their idea.

CLASS

Crowdfunding: What Is It?

Crowdfunding is simply getting money for an idea from the same audience that you expect will use your product; these same people, you hope, will be excited enough about using the product to pay ahead of time and tell others to do the same. Crowdfunding comes in two categories: funding for a cause, and funding for a product. For products, this can be further divided into two types of crowdfunding: rewards and equity. We will be looking at the rewards type of crowdfunding. Equity is more about small investments in a company to help it launch, and strikes me as a bit out of the purview of libraries. On the other hand, you may want to look up and familiarize yourself with AngelList or EquityNet, as these may come up with patrons. For the most part, though, our concern will be with cause crowdfunding.

Which Site is Best for You?

Once you have your audience you will want to ask about their ideas. This will give you a chance to discover who has actually thought about how to sell an idea. Some people may have a very vague and long-winded idea. Ask them for their "elevator pitch." An elevator pitch is a 30-second persuasive description of their idea. This class is organized around causes, and if a patron says that he or she is not trying to *sell* anything, but rather want people to *give* or *donate*, explain that he or she is trying to sell the idea that it is worth giving or donating to a cause.

If patrons do not have an elevator pitch, take a few minutes to let them come up with one. If they do not have it written down, ask the patrons to write it out before giving the pitch to each other. Most of these crowdfunding websites will require a *short description*. The elevator pitch and short description can be one and the same. Once the patrons are ready to explain their pitches, it is a good idea to go around the room and have them share what they are trying to do.

Once each patron has shared an idea, you can let him or her know which site is best for that idea.

GoFundMe

WHAT DOES IT RAISE MONEY FOR? GoFundMe is for personal causes. Some examples are a person who needs an operation he or she cannot afford, or helping someone avoid foreclosure, or even funding a vacation. Of course, common sense dictates that no one is going to give you money for a vacation unless there is a good reason, but if a local volunteer wishes for a well-deserved break and a trip to the Bahamas, this is the site to use. The strength of GoFundMe is that it is more of a platform for people who know each other, rather than a promotional tool. Think of it as the digital version of a collection jar sitting on the counter at your local store.

Take the patron to this site: https://www.gofundme.com/success. The stories change from time to time, but the site has successful campaigns on that people can use for guidance to decide if their cause is best addressed on this site.

WHAT WILL IT TAKE TO USE? GoFundMe donations are considered personal gifts, so anyone can use the platform. Users will need an email account, and must give their real name. It is also important to use GoFundMe's WePay account, which will require bank and routing number information. If you are raising money for someone else, that person can be invited to download the money using the same information.

GoFundMe does not impose a time limit on a campaign. The user can leave the campaign running until it reaches its goals. However, within 30 days of starting a campaign, money must be withdrawn from the WePay account. It is important to do this, or otherwise the funds may be returned. There is also a 7.9 percent handling fee plus a 30-cent charge for every donation; 5 percent of this goes to GoFundMe, and the remainder to WePay.

To actually create a campaign, the patron only needs a goal, a title, and a category for their campaign. They must choose a category from GoFundMe's options; you will notice from the figure on page XX that Business & Entrepreneurs is one option. Although there is overlap with the various Crowdfunding platforms, it is good to remember that each has different reputations and strengths.

Once patrons have named and categorized their campaigns, they need to load a photo or link to a video on YouTube or Vimeo. They can then tell their stories—again, this will be a short description or elevator pitch. The final step is to share the campaign on FB and link to their social media to promote the campaign.

WHAT WILL IT TAKE TO MAKE FUNDRAISING SUCCESSFUL? Now is a good time to ask your patrons if they are thinking of using this platform. If they are, ask them to read their elevator pitch again. Ask the other patrons to give feedback: Does it sound good? How does it compare to the success stories on the GoFundMe page? (Feel free to go back and listen again to any that you think are relevant.) There is not much information on a GoFundMe page, so what little there is must have impact. Hopefully, the other patrons will provide input on how to make their story one that gets donations.

You also noticed that video is an option. Photos and videos will play a big part in the success of one of these campaigns. It is not likely that the person in your class will have a photo ready to show, but you can ask the other patrons and give your own opinions on what kinds of photos or videos would be appropriate.

CROWDRISE CrowdRise is basically a GoFundMe for charitable organizations. The main difference is that when you set up your event or cause, you will designate a certified charity as the recipient. CrowdRise recognizes over 15 million charities, so finding one should not be a problem. In times of disaster, like the earthquake in Haiti, the site provides a good way to contribute beyond cutting a check.

Kickstarter

WHAT DOES IT RAISE MONEY FOR? Compared to GoFundMe, Kickstarter is more about creating an item or an event. It is often used for creating games, a work of art, an art performance, or a piece of technology. One of the more interesting uses of Kickstarter was to raise the money to create potato salad. Zack "Danger" Brown started a campaign for $60 dollars to learn to make potato salad. He ended up raising over $55,000.

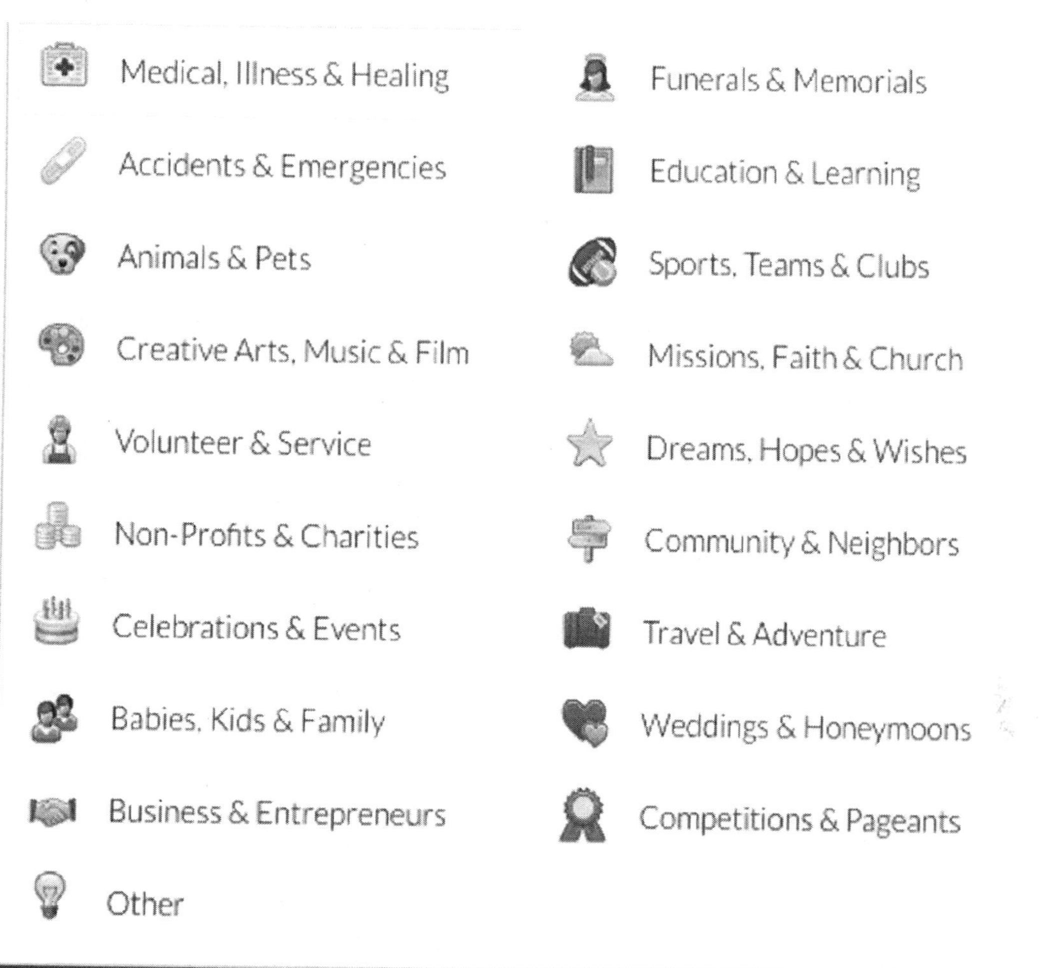

A GoFundMe project needs to be placed into a category so contributors can discover it.

Not all Kickstarters are as successful or as amusing, but this gives you an idea of how off-the-wall requests can take on a life of their own on Kickstarter.

You can take your patrons to the site's Projects We Love page to view some of the current projects: https://www.kickstarter.com/discover/recommended. After viewing the projects, you should explain to your patrons that Kickstarter has some rules:

- Users must create something that can be shared
- The project must be honest and clearly presented, which basically means do not show a product that you have not actually made yet. A lot of tech inventions were started on Kickstarter, and this is the main site for that sort of crowdfunding. So if your idea is to create a flying car, don't create an animation of a flying car and say you can build one.
- Kickstarter is not for charities (charities can use GoFundMe though!)
- Do not offer equity—no building something for part ownership of the item.
- No prohibited items (illegal, unregulated, or dangerous): see https://www.kickstarter.com/rules/prohibited?ref=rules.

WHAT WILL IT TAKE TO USE THE SITE? Share with your patrons that Kickstarter is a little more in depth than GoFundMe. The basics are the same; users will need an email account and password to create a Kickstarter account under your real name. Once you have an account, you must:

- Choose a category
- Title your project
- Load an image or video
- Create a short description
- Set a funding goal
- Have banking information to link to

These requirements are the same for GoFundMe. In addition, users will need to:

- Designate a location for the project
- Set a duration (although Kickstarter prefers 30 days, I have seen projects on there for 60 days) and an end time.

The story part of Kickstarter is more involved than for GoFundMe. First, almost all Kickstarter projects have a video. These demonstrate the prototype or show the type of item you're planning on building. The description is about the same, but there is also an option to request help from the community, and a Risk and Challenges section.

These sections allow people supporting a Kickstarter to volunteer skills and knowledge, as well as money. Kickstarter is trying to create and foster its own community on their site. The idea of allowing skills and explaining the risks and challenges is an effort to help people be more involved in the projects they are supporting. In the same vein, there is much more to your profile than in GoFundMe, including areas for an image and a biography.

The biggest difference between the two sites is Kickstarter's rewards system. Every Kickstarter project offers rewards to the supporters. Rewards must be set at different levels of donation, so one reward for $1, another reward for $5, and so on must be determined, with increasing values for both the rewards and the donations.

WHAT WILL IT TAKE TO MAKE FUNDRAISING SUCCESSFUL? A successful Kickstarter campaign is a little more difficult and a little more involved than a GoFundMe campaign. The most obvious issue is the fact that patrons will need to set up a rewards system. These rewards are usually some sort of tangible thing, such as a hat with a logo, a poster, or one of the first products off the line. Our example of the potato salad project provided a copy of the recipe and an actual bowl of the potato salad he was making. Far from just amusing, though, these rewards need to be thought out and have some actual value for a successful Kickstarter.

The other elements of the biography and the description and video also need to be well considered.

Reward #1

0 backers

Title	
Pledge amount	$0
Description	+ Add an item
Estimated delivery	Select month / Select year
Shipping details	Select an option
Limit availability	☐ Enable reward limit

Duplicate reward   X Delete

+ Add a new reward

Kickstarter uses rewards to incentivize larger contributions. A little thought about rewards will increase returns.

These are the elements that will "sell" the Kickstarter project to the public. If any of your patrons have identified Kickstarter as a possible platform to launch a project, have them provide ideas for making the project more appealing. Take suggestions from other members of the class to help them.

Other Crowdfunding Sites to Think About

There are a few more sites worth looking into. Crowdfunding has become very popular over the past 10 years, and it is hard to discuss all platforms, but here are some that may more closely conform to your patrons' needs.

- RocketHub is one of the largest crowdfunding platforms, and serves as more of a community and support for entrepreneurs than the others. It allows for a campaign to raise funds, not just for an item but for an organization, or to create a product.
- StartSomeGood is a platform for social innovation. A cross between GoFundMe and Kickstarter, it specializes in one-off campaigns for events, items, or causes that support social good in the world.
- Patreon is an odd bird. It is set up so that artists can get monthly funds for creating arts—literally attracting art patrons. The artist will set up an account not unlike crowdsourcing sites, and he or she can specify whether funds are received monthly or after a certain piece is created. The artist is under no obligation to create, or give away their work; it is merely a way for people to feel like they are funding the work of artists.

HOW THE TOPIC CAME UP AND BECAME A CLASS

This project was started with a friend who had run a successful Kickstarter project. I talked him into helping with a need at the library, and he came in and walked us through what he had done. He also told us about GoFundMe. Dealing with an economically challenged population, I saw interest in crowdfunding. I went over the differences and saw how it would be possible to create a crowdfunding page, but not for the library. In preparing a presentation for our library's Friends organization, I thought, "Hey, I could take this right to the patrons too." We often deal with people who could benefit from this service. More like a seminar than a class, I have used this information to get people pointed in the right direction for crowdfunding and have them come to the library for support when they needed specifics such as copy editing or help with images.

Part II

PROGRAMS FOR THE MILLENNIAL LIFESTYLE

A question I still hear regarding libraries is its relevance to modern life. Especially for teens and tweens, the library primarily means a place to get that source that is not online for a paper or project. We know we're relevant, but how do we prove it to the skeptics? One way is to introduce classes on technology, but more importantly, introduce workshops on technology that reach beyond job searching, office skills, and social media. Patrons are more than likely to have other classes or friends who can teach those skills. Rather than repeat offerings by other organizations, we can branch out to offer more "trendy" or "frivolous" things.

I am certain that making motion GIFs is not considered a necessary digital literacy skill per se, but it is one way that people can create. The web is defined in this point in time by the average person's ability to create content and publish it to expand their sphere of influence. In the bigger picture, this is a good gateway to digital literacy. More importantly, a class like this one can be a gateway for people to discover their voice.

Some of these classes are geared to a young adult audience, but that is mostly because this is the audience who seeks to create. I think that, if you found the right group of patrons, any of these classes could be taught to any age group.

Make Your Meme Move

Motion GIFs

WHY BOTHER?

Memes are popular among social media users, and are a great introduction to the basics of working with images.

Motion GIFs are also a good introduction to the basics of video and animation. There are some online tools we can explore. Motion GIFs are a little more difficult, and making these gives patrons a chance to explore some of the basics of video making. These classes are not offered because the skills learned are super valuable, but because helping patrons create content, no matter how ephemeral, is good for them and therefore good for the library.

Remember, "I can haz cheezburger" and "All your base are belong to us" mean that proper grammar and spelling are not required for a meme. ***http://www.relatably.com/m/img/most-popular-memes-ever/***

WHAT PATRONS WILL NEED

- Basic computer skills
- A FB account or Instagram account
- Images

WHAT YOU WILL NEED

- Ability to display an active computer screen (projector monitor or enough room for everyone to gather around)
- An open Internet connection
- Images to change

> **PRO TIP**
>
> **Program 11 in this book, on searching for images, can be used with this program. Memes would most likely be safe under the satire clause of Fair Use laws, but it is always a good idea to cover copyrights.**

Remember, memes can be considered protected speech as satire.

OUTLINE

1. Make a Meme with imgflip
   a. Image
      i. Online or your own
      ii. Resolution
   b. Caption an image
   c. Options
2. Make an animated GIF
   a. Select an image
   b. Design the GIF
      i. Frame rate
      ii. Resolution and other options
3. Sharing with Others

THE BIG PICTURE

The reason for a class can be simply fun, and because you can. Everyone on FB has seen a meme or two that we thought were funny. They are easy to make and share. In addition, meme creation is a good launching point to introduce people to some basic computer information, and promote your programs at the same time. I built this class as a way to promote itself, but don't feel like you need to do so. The class will teach patrons to load or find images online, and add text or motion to create an animated GIF for FB or other social media.

Sometimes a short class can be just fun for the people who participate, and you can teach them some of the underlying concepts of computers by explaining why small GIF files are easy to share and store.

CLASS

You should introduce the patrons to memes. Now this can be dicey, as the nature of memes is the combination of humor and opinion, and what one person finds funny can offend another. So you should probably pick out some "safe" memes beforehand. One suggestion is cat memes, because the Internet runs on cats.

Image

The first step is getting your patrons to choose an image.

ONLINE OR YOUR OWN IMAGE In all likelihood, patrons will not have brought an image. You could have the patrons search for an image, or provide some if they did not bring their own image. Again, the suggestion here is provide some for them. If a patron has an image, this can be used. It can be funny to caption a home image as well.

RESOLUTION If patrons bring images, it is advisable to talk a little about resolution, as their images are more than likely too large if taken with a camera phone or digital camera. There is more information on this in program 2 and other programs in this book, but here you can briefly explain that video for monitors is roughly 150 pixels per inch, which means that a 600 × 600 pixel image will be 4" by 4" on a high-resolution monitor. However, it could be as large as 8" by 8" on a standard monitor.

> **PRO TIP**
>
> **If they want to use their own images, you can show patrons how to downsize the images with something like PhotoCat or, better yet, sign them up and run that class as well.**

Photos taken with a cell phone or a point-and-shoot camera are *huge* in terms of video. Point-and-shoots were designed to have images printed at 1200 pixels per inch, and phone cameras were made to compete with point-and-shoots. An 8-megapixel camera on a phone is not uncommon; that would be 3266 by 2450 pixels, or 24 by 25 inches on a regular screen. For sanity's sake,

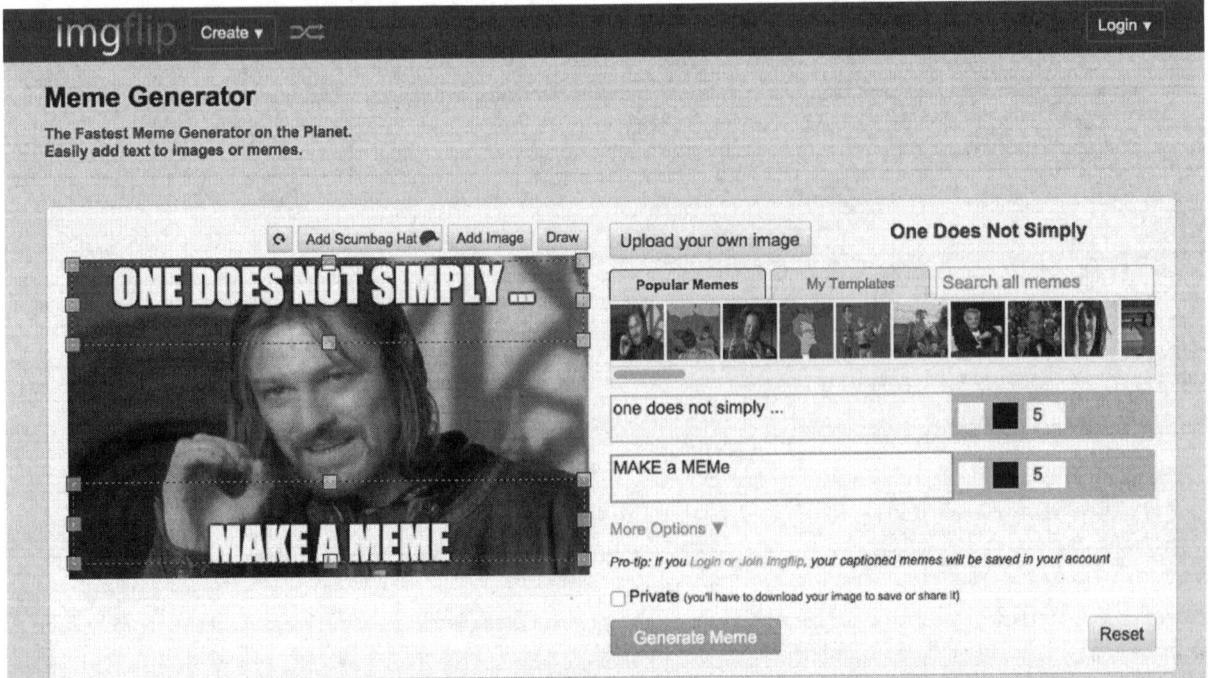

In imgflip, text can be easily added in the interface.

we will run this class by using one of the memes offered by the imgflip site. When we create motion GIFs, there will be more discussion about this.

CAPTION AN IMAGE There are number of online sources for creating memes and GIFs; the one we will use is called imgflip. It can be a used without creating an account, but the site does allow users to create accounts and share their work. Other options are Memepile (http://www.memepile.com/) and Caption.iT (http://www.caption.it/).

1. Go to https://imgflip.com/.
2. Click on Make a Meme on the right-hand side.
3. Choose your image. You can choose to import your own, or simply use one of the ones popular right now.
4. You will notice a series of boxes to the right of the image; that is where text is entered (see the figure below).
5. The white box is the default text color; click on it to see other available options, and you can also add hex colors. (Check out http://www.w3schools.com/colors/colors_picker.asp to find other colors.)
6. The box next to color is the shadow color and weight. The color of the shadow can be changed like the text color, and the shadow density changed.
7. Type in your text and click Generate Meme.
8. The meme will appear in its own box

Creating a meme is pretty easy to do; mind you, the tricky part is making them funny. Let the patrons share what they have done with each other, or display them to the room. There is the option at the bottom of the page to share your meme across social media. To share, simply click on the appropriate social media icon. The image link can also be used by FB and social media. Sharing on FB will open another tab in your browser. My suggestion is to have the patrons do this if they are logged into their account. This is also a good opportunity to get patrons to follow the library's social media and share information about the library.

The link is also useful if the patrons DO NOT wish to share and would like to be able to retrieve their memes. The Bulletin Board Code (BBCode) and img HTML have code to display memes on web pages and embed them in blog sites.

Don't close the page; we will explore the options on the Meme Generator and set up the motion GIF part. Have your patrons:

1. Copy the link and paste it in the address bar of a new tab.
2. From there, right-click on the image and have them save the image to their desktop or laptop computer.

PRO TIP

Shadow and text color default to white, which will work for most images. But if you want to step it up, pull out a color wheel and show the patrons how light on dark works, or how complimentary colors work (for example, yellow against blue or red with green). This web page has a good color calculator.

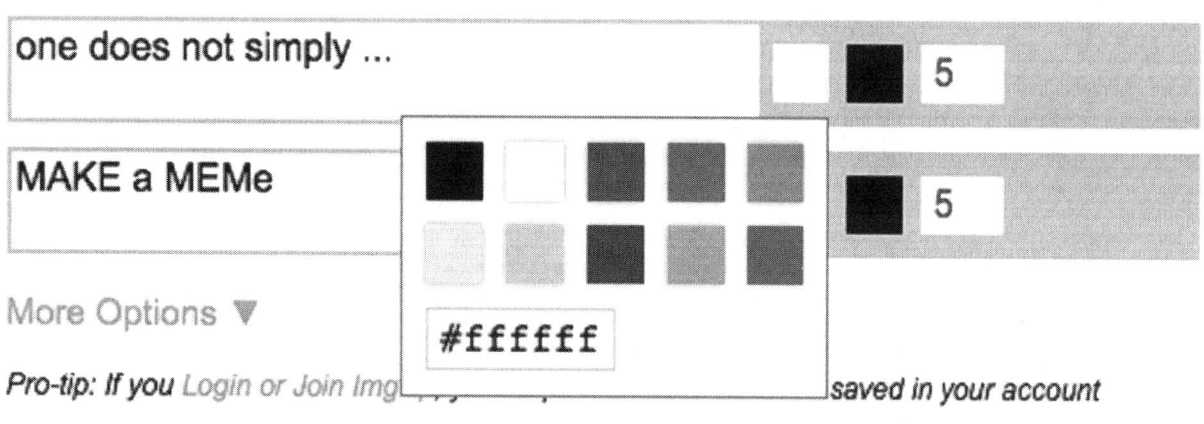

imgflip has the basic color tools to customize your meme.

Memes can be shared on social networks directly from imgflip.

OPTIONS Click on the Change Settings button to take the patrons back to the image. Across the top of the image is a series of options: the first arrow is for rotation, while the third will let you add an image inside your image. The fourth will let you draw on the image. The third option is a fun opportunity to add your library's logo to the meme, so that when patrons share it, they will spread word about the class and like classes.

> **PRO TIP**
>
> **If you have a library logo and you can use it, have your patrons add it to this second picture. Imgflip will take PNGs so if you have one that has a transparency, it can be added like a logo to the images.**

Under the text boxes are More Options. Click on this, and a new dialog box will open.

1. Have the patrons click on the Add Text box. This will add a third text box to the meme. In the next text box that appears, have them add: I made this @ [Your Library]. The text will appear in the center box.
2. The other options will affect *all* text boxes.
   a. Font changes the font.
   b. Max Font Size will shrink the font, which is good if your text is crowding out the image.
   c. Unchecking the Font Shadow box will remove the shadow
   d. Use All Caps will change the text to caps in the text boxes.
   e. Enable drag/drop & resize lets you move the text boxes around like you would in Microsoft Word.

Now have your patrons move the text and play with these options to see what they do. When they have something they like, generate the meme, and repeat the process to save their meme to their desktop. If you have a logo and can use it, have them add it to this image!

Make an Animated GIF

There are two ways to make a GIF. One is to string a series of pictures together, and the other is to import a video that will loop. We will focus on images. Go back to the imgflip home page or choose the drop-down menu and select Make a GIF from Images. If you went to the home page, then click on Make a GIF on the menu on the right.

SELECT AND IMPORT IMAGE Now the patron should have two images saved to the desktop.

1. Have patrons click the Upload Images button, and import both images.
2. When the first one is loaded, a series of options will appear on the right; ignore these.
3. When the second is loaded, you will see the image flash between the two.
   a. This is the loop! An animated GIFs loop means that the images run through, and then start again from the beginning.
4. Have the patrons scroll down below the image to see that there is an Auto Arrange.
   a. This is the Timeline; it is both the order of images and a place to edit the images.
   b. Have your patrons reload their first image; it will appear on the timeline after the second image they loaded.
   c. Look at the preview at the top left of the animated GIF. The time has changed, and it seems like the first image lasts longer. It does because it loops.
   d. Now have the patron drag the second version of the first image to the right after the first; you will not see a change in the preview, but this displays the image a second time, and then the second image with the extra text.

PRO TIP

You are really moving into video editing with this program and the timeline. This is a good way to explain some of the basics of video editing, such as the frame rate and timeline. You can have the patrons change text color, add other images, to make a more complex GIF.

DESIGN THE GIF The loop will play the two identical images, and then the image with extra text. It is important to generate it this way because the loop will start at the first image when it loads to a page! Patrons can add other elements to the GIF, importing images and sliding in new ones. You can even allow them to redraw on it.

Now have the patrons play with the timing by sliding the delay at the top right of the Options menu.

1. Take the Delay up to 1000, this is 1 second.
2. You will notice that the image at the end lasts longer before it changes, but all three images are displaying for 1 second.
3. You can have your patrons reimport the first image if they would like it to last longer, or the second. I think it works best with 3 seconds of the meme without the library text, and then the library text for 1 second.

PRO TIP

We were talking about this class as a good segue into video production. It can also be an introduction to animations. If you have ever created a flipbook, you can do that and scan the images into a computer or take a picture of them. Then load the images to this program to make a cartoon GIF. This can be a fun class for young adult audiences.

RESOLUTION AND OTHER OPTIONS Earlier in the class, we talked about resolution and why size is important when displaying images on a screen. With GIFs, these are doubly important, as moving GIFs are popular in part because they are an easy way to share video clips, and replace video on social media sites. This is because file size affects the load time. You will notice that we have only three images in the GIF; high-resolution video has 60 frames per second (or fps), and standard video has 30 fps. High-resolution image size is 1920 × 1080; standard size is 720 × 480. These factors make video files larger and harder to share. There are a few options for making the files smaller. They will not matter because you are using web images, but going over this detail explains a lot.

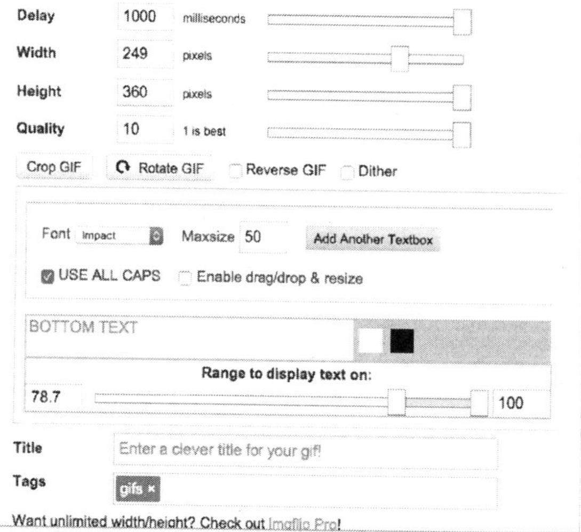

imgflip will allow you to shrink image and file size from the motion screens.

- If you look at the options below Delay you will see Width and Height. Although these can be changed independently, if you shrink one, you should shrink the other.
- Quality (set to 10 by default) will make the images crisper, but also larger and harder to load.
- Crop GIF will let you make an image smaller or larger without changing the size. (Be careful using this if you have loaded more than one image, as the crop operates on one image at a time.)
- Rotate GIF may be important if a patron loads his or her own images. It also will let you rotate multiple times; an image can be flipped upside down by rotating it twice.
- Dither will make the edges smoother
- The Dialog box below them is for text, and is almost identical to the Meme one, except there is a *range to display text*. This option will place text on the image. If there are 10 images on the Timeline, and you set it from 15 to 50, it would display the text from halfway through the second image to the end of the fifth image (my suggestion is to let the patrons do the math).
- Title is self-explanatory.
- Tags should be obvious to a librarian.

- The rest are options only available to imgflip pro users.

You can come back to this section later by using the Change Settings button to return to this screen. Let the patrons play with the image and options. There is a reset button on the right; it will, however, erase everything, so do not use it.

Sharing with Others

Have the patrons click the Generate GIF button; the dialog box that opens is almost identical to the Meme Share box. The importance difference here is that you can download the GIF directly. Ideally, you can have your patrons post their motion GIFs, as these were designed to promote the library. However, if they don't want to share their GIFs on their social media, ask them to add a tag with their name, download the file, and share it on your library's social media. Replace @ [Your Library] with by [Patron Name] @ [Your Library], then share the best.

> **PRO TIP**
>
> **Teens and tweens are more likely to use Instagram and, as of 2016, use Snapchat more than FB. It is worth using these social media platforms to present this program.**

HOW THE TOPIC CAME UP AND BECAME A CLASS

When working at the library, you always see a few kids who are bored,[1] waiting for their parents to finish applying for jobs or researching something. One day I had a disagreement about whether animated GIFs had transparency or not (they can be transparent but do not have transparency, and if that doesn't make sense, don't worry about it, as this is a big ongoing argument you don't want in your life). I started playing with some GIF generators in a video game creation program to prove my point, and one of those kids, one of my regulars, saw me doing this and thought it was cool. Now, the program was expensive, but he just wanted to make a basic motion GIF, to make a meme. We sat doing some of those, and then I found a motion GIF site for him play on. The experience made me understand that creating a meme was a good way to teach animation and sizing, and teaching kids how to make motion GIFs was basically part of teaching animation for video games. So I would often show people, kids and adults, how to do this as a lark in the computer lab.

NOTE

1. Kellen Beck, "Snapchat Is Now the Most Popular Social Network among Teens, According to New Study." Mashable, April 14, 2016. http://mashable.com/2016/04/14/snapchat-teens-winner/#pQLQrw5ryiqz.

Making Web Comics

Why Not?

WHY BOTHER?

Why do the class? Well, why not? It is a good way to get children and preteens working on computers. It will give your library a class to offer younger audiences, and pave the way for children to do more with technology as a creative medium rather than acting as passive consumers. On a more basic level, though, we are placing graphic items on a two-dimensional plane. In doing this, we are working with layout and balance and doing many of the basic skills needed when using Microsoft Publisher, PowerPoint, and Adobe InDesign. In addition, by creating a comic strip, we are touching on the basics of narrative structure. The idea of building a story is pretty empowering, no matter how simple it is.

WHAT PATRONS WILL NEED

- Basic computer skills
- A usable email address (not necessarily access)

WHAT YOU WILL NEED

- Ability to display an active computer screen (projector monitor or enough room for everyone to gather around)
- An open Internet connection
- Digital images to change

OUTLINE

1. Preparing to make a comic
   a. Picking a comic
   b. Choosing a platform and hosting
      i. ToonDoo and others
2. Making a comic on ToonDoo
   a. Choosing a layout
   b. Choosing backgrounds, characters, and objects
   c. Laying out a scene
      i. Modifying objects and characters
      ii. Adding text
3. Making your own comic
   a. Using TraitR
   b. Loading an image in ImagineR

THE BIG PICTURE

Web comics are not something that is considered in standard digital literacy, but they offer an easy way to empower young people to add something to the web. The main concepts covered in this class are:

- A little narrative theory
- Content creation and hosting
- Graphic concepts

Web comics can be very fun, but most are geared for adults. Instead of worrying about showing actual comics, this is a good time to bring in books and comics from the library collection. This class will create a web comic, selecting a series of items from a list that is pretty standard across programs. The icons themselves are fairly unique to web comics, and there is an opportunity to customize characters to match the patron and import backgrounds, including one of the library.

CLASS

When you teach this class, especially with a younger audience, giving them time to create is problematic.

> **PRO TIP**
>
> **If your library has an anime or manga club, this could be a good activity for them, or could be a way to create interest in joining the club.**

Although a comic seems a simple thing, I have found that teaching creative work, especially to audiences under the age of 11, hard to do. My suggestion for starting this is to give them a comic to emulate. You may have a good idea of which comic to start with; it would be best to find something popular with your audience.

Picking a Comic

So the first step is to pick a comic for the audience. The younger the audience, the easier the comic should be. A single-panel comic can be used, or a multiple-panel comic strip. I am not sure how many kids still read comics in newspapers, but this could be a good chance to introduce them to Charlie Brown, Heathcliff, or even Bloom County. You could choose three or four of your favorite comics for them and let them decide which one to use. I will point out that ToonDoo will not have the actual characters of your comics, or the backgrounds or the props; it just provides a premade template to start with.

If you want to try something that might be more recognizable for your patrons, you can try a graphic novel or manga. In either case, you need to find a simpler panel for character or actions, as the options for either will be limited. If you choose to do a manga, choose an easier page for your panel template. If you need more than four panels, do more than one comic. The creative part of this class is trying to create the comic with the more limited tools of ToonDoo. While the primary goal is to create a comic, the lesson also discusses the structure of comics.

> **PRO TIP**
>
> **You should download some "sound effects" bubbles before the program.**

Start by discussing the comic. You can ask patrons what is going on in the comic. Ask about how they understand anger, or what the various elements are. A good primer is to have them identify:

- Panels: the individual cells of a comic
- Tiers: a row of panels

Classic elements of comics include onomatopoeic words like Pow! or Whammy.

- Word balloons: the shapes used to suggest speech
- Captions: words that serve as narration or exposition in comics
- "Sound effects": onomatopoeic words to suggest noises
- Props: items in a comic
- Characters
    - Explore how characters' "body" language works with the words[1]

> **PRO TIP**
>
> **If you have an urge to explore more about comics with the class or on your own, two books to look into are *Understanding Comics and Comics and Sequential Art* (see the note at the end of this chapter). Both or either will give you a good grounding for this class and a deeper understanding on what is a disappearing art form.**

Choosing a Platform and Hosting your Comic

Web comics are slowly going out of fashion, and are not as popular as they once were. There used to be quite a few platforms for creating web comics. Oddly, for such a simple idea—adding images to panels—comic creation programs do not have a lot of similarity in terms of their layout or interface. When you choose one, you really need to stay with the program or learn a new one completely. For this program, I focus on ToonDoo (http://www.toondoo.com). Much of the interface skills and features do not translate to the other major web creator, Make Beliefs Comix (http://www.makebeliefscomix.com) or Stripgenerator (http://stripgen

erator.com/). However, a web comic could be made in any basic layout program, including Microsoft Word. There are even some special message boards dedicated to web comics, but it may be just as fun to post them to an Instagram or Snapchat page.

Log into ToonDoo

The first thing you need to do when you log into ToonDoo is create a user account. Like most sites, it will ask for an email account. Luckily this does not mean you will have to verify it, so any previously unused email account is fine for a class. There is, however, an option for an institutional license if you believe it will be a problem.

In general I could see no purpose for this unless:

- You plan on running this activity a lot
- You feel that a modified closed board would get use
- You feel that there is a reason to have discussion about the web comics

The main ToonDoo menu is in the upper-left corner.

Make a Comic on ToonDoo

Once your patrons create an account and join ToonDoo, they will select Create a Toon from the menu. Toons is the first menu item, and Create a Toon is the first item when the menu drops down. You can familiarize the patrons with a few of these items at the beginning:

- Create Toon is where we create a web comic.
- My ToonDoos is where the completed web comics will be stored and available for editing.
- The remaining options have to do with web comics hosted on the site. I would ask patrons not to explore these until completing the first part of this project.

Choosing a Layout

When you select Create Toon, the program automatically takes you to the layout screen. These layouts are pretty standard across comics, and users should not have a problem finding a comic format. You will want to walk the patrons through picking a layout like the one you have selected.

Again, mangas and graphic novels may have more panels than the maximum of four; some will have six or eight panels per page. If you want to do a comic that doesn't fit this size, you can always put two or more comics together as a final product.

PRO TIP

The final output from this class can be printed out. When choosing a layout, have patrons think about what the comic will look like printed out, and have a color printer handy. These can be hung up for the patrons or taken home.

Choosing Backgrounds, Characters, and Objects

The next screen is where the bulk of the layout will be done. Backgrounds, characters, and objects will be found in the item menu. The overall layout of the screen includes:

- Item menu on the left
- Options for various items open in the center, to the right of the item menu
- Page or layout on the right
- Toolbar at the bottom
- The tabs to call up the DoodleR, TraitR and ImagineR interfaces are at the bottom, to the right of the toolbar (more on those later)

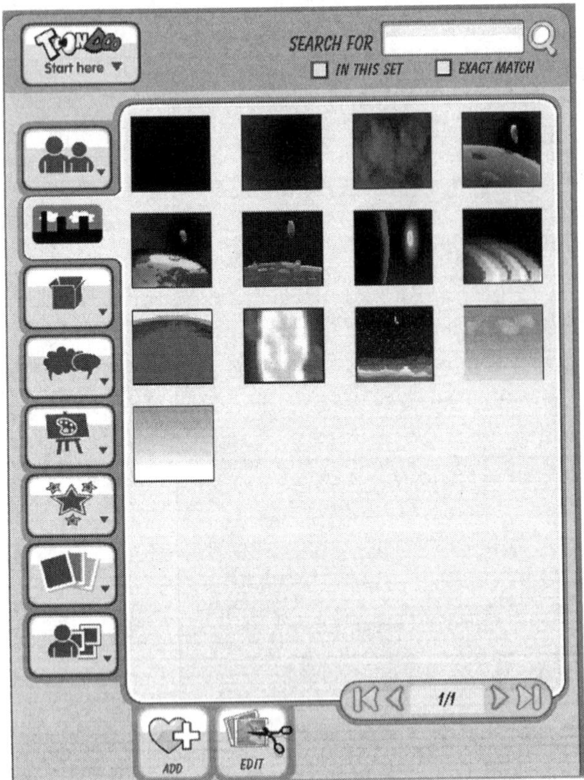

ToonDoo has limited, but useful backgrounds.

The process for creating backgrounds, characters, and objects are all very similar. They are also very simple. It should not take patrons long to pick up, since the basic operation is drag and drop.

The second item from the top on the menu is the Background option. Clicking on this opens a pop-up with eight choices: Scenery, Space, Abstract, Fantasy, Indoors, Outdoors, Landmarks, and Sports.

You will notice that once you select a category, a series of options will inhabit the center screen, like the figure above. Show your patrons that some categories have multiple pages of choices, and clicking on the arrows at the bottom of that window can access the options. Whatever comic you selected is unlikely to have an exact match for the background, so just have them choose whatever they feel. The patrons can simply click on their choice and drag it over to the frame.

The next item to work on is Characters, the top option on the item menu. Some characters have multiple poses in the options. Tell the patrons not to get sidetracked by these options, but rather just choose a character to work with and drag and drop it into the frame.

This ToonDoo menu will let you modify the cartoon characters.

Finally, patrons can place any props they like into the frames. Props are the third item on the menu. The background automatically positions itself behind the characters and props. The character(s) and props will be positioned in the order that they are placed. If patrons want to change their positions, they can do so next.

Layout of a Scene

With several items in the frame, we can now work with the layout. You may notice that a prop is as large as a character, or two characters are crowded into a frame. The toolbar will allow users to change that. All the objects in the frame can still be selected by clicking on them; you can tell these are selected by the dotted line that appears around them (I call this the selection area).

Shrink and Enlarge buttons are for changing the size of an object, a character, and even the background (this is useful if you want to zoom in on a character reaction). The To Front and To Back buttons place the object either in the front or in the back of the frame. Front and back are *absolute*, meaning if you have four items in a frame, and they are in the order 1, 2, 3, and 4, selecting 4 and choosing To Back will place it behind 1, so the order would be 4, 1, 2, and 3. If you want the order to be 1, 2, 4, and 3, it would be easier to select 3 and click on To Front. It is also important to tell patrons that if they have problems selecting an object, the selection area marked by the dotted line may be covering the smaller object, and make it necessary to change the order to place the larger object in the rear.

Modifying Objects and Characters

When the characters and objects are arranged, you can explore some other options on the toolbar. Clone will copy, Flip will reverse the image, and Rotate will turn the selection in the direction of the arrow on the toolbar. Use these tools to modify how the characters

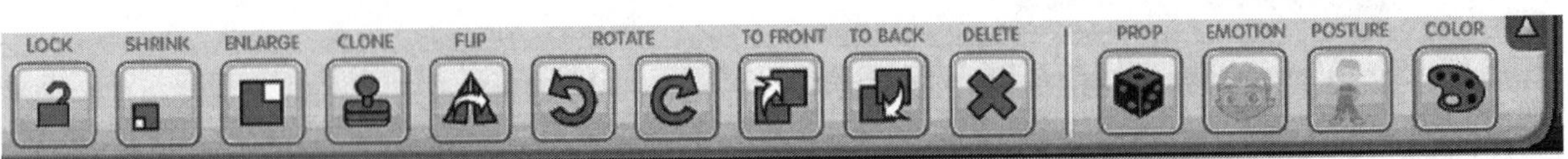

On the bottom of the ToonDoo page is the image manipulation menu.

are relating to each other. Remember to look at the original comic and observe how the characters are drawn to relate to each other and to convey emotion. Use size and rotation to get the characters to relate to each other, their surroundings, and their props.

You will notice that the final four items on the toolbar are sometimes "grayed out," based on whether that option is available.

- Return to your character
- Find a character that will change its posture
- Find a character that will change its emotion
- Let the patrons find other postures and emotions that suit the chosen cartoon

Adding Text

The final step is what makes the images a cartoon—adding text balloons. The Text Balloon option is the fourth menu item. When you place a balloon, it will prompt you for text. Leave text for when you display the final cartoon, so patrons can copy the text letter for letter.

If you have the ability, you should take a few minutes to let patrons share with each other what they have done. I always like to project it on a large screen if I can, but that is not always possible. With a smaller class, walking from station to station will work.

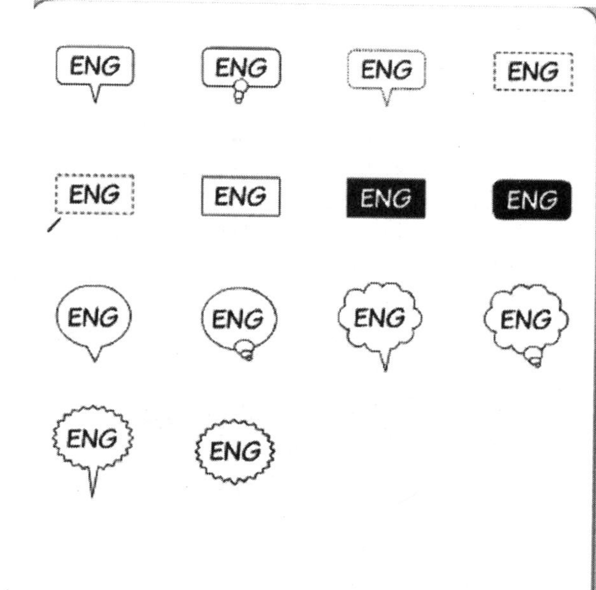

ToonDoo's thought and word bubbles provide classic elements of cartoon art.

When you are ready to save, the normal file options are under the ToonDoo logo in the upper-left corner of the screen. You can save your cartoon there. The interface will allow you to Publish, Share with Friends, or Keep Private. It also will let you print the image if you have a color printer handy.

Saving and opening web toons is done through the main menu of ToonDoo.

PRO TIP

If you are interested in making this a theme class, you could load in advance some characters that your patrons would know—historical figures for a certain day, or the appropriate background for a book club you are working with. By using the ImagineR tool, it is very easy to bring a specific character or setting into a comic.

Making Your Own Comic

It would be a pretty bad class if we just copied someone else's work. The next step is to make your own comic. There are some pretty nonsensical characters and fun backgrounds in ToonDoo, so you can let the patrons run wild at this point. However, there are two features that could make this a lot more fun. If you have the time left in your class (you probably know that the younger and larger the audience, the longer it takes to get through), you can try two other features.

Using TraitR

At the bottom of the toolbar is the TraitR interface; if you click on this, you will get the interface in the figure below. The interface may be more familiar to your students than it is to you, as it is similar to many avatar-generating programs in services like the Wii or Xbox Live. The character is shown in the center box, and can be zoomed in or out and the stance adjusted using the controls directly under the character. The top row on the right controls the features. Note that the male and female bodies are separate, with the male on the top row and the female on the bottom. Under these options are controls for the eyes and mouth. They are separate for a reason.

1. Select the features you wish the character to have.
2. Once the features are selected, you can modify their dimensions under the image.
3. You may change their facial features.
4. When you have completed a character, save it by naming it and then clicking Save at the bottom.
5. After saving you will return to the web comic creation interface, but now your gallery has your character in it. The posture and expression tools will work for this character.

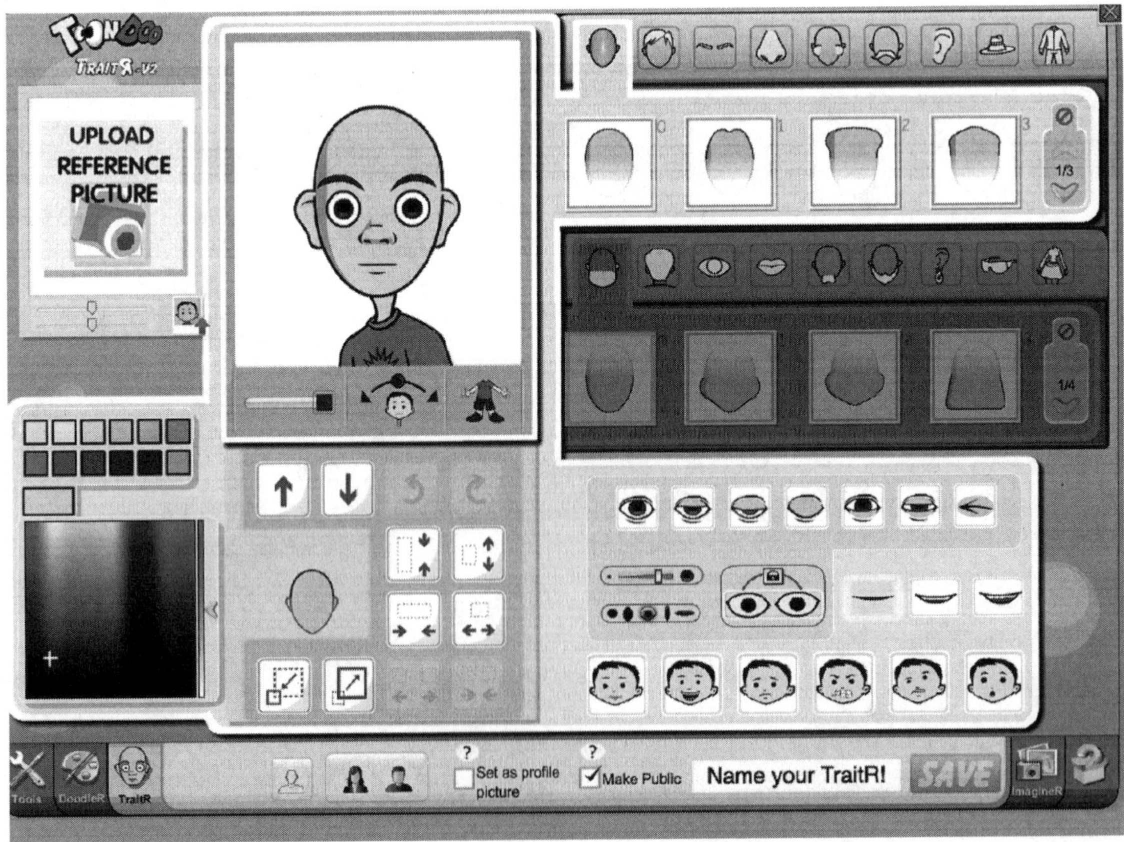

ToonDoo's most complicated interface is the Character Customization.

Loading an Image in ImagineR

The other feature worth exploring is ImagineR, which will also allow you to bring custom content to a web comic. Your images will also appear in your gallery for later use. You can easily load an image of a location and use it for background—perhaps an image of your library. I suggest using *smaller* images; the site tends to lag on larger ones. Another suggestion is loading PNG files of item from the web to use for props.

How the Topic Came Up and Became a Class

I had not intended to teach web comics, but was working with some young patrons who were very interested in mangas and graphic novels. I found the ToonDoo program to make a flyer for their graphic novel/anime club. Using the TraitR and ImagineR tools, we played pretty fast and loose with copyright, and made a decent flyer. I ended up showing them how to make the flyer. So, when I was thinking about multimedia classes, I thought this would be a good one to squeeze in—simple, fast, and pretty painless, but with a final object they can print out and take home.

NOTE

1. Scott McCloud, *Understanding Comics* (New York: HarperPerennial, 1994); Will Eisner, *Comics and Sequential Art: Principles and Practices from the Legendary Cartoonist* (New York: W. W. Norton, 2008).

Share Your Songs, Find an Audience

SoundCloud, Audiomack, and Bandcamp

WHY BOTHER?

What do artists do when they need to find an audience or get themselves heard? "Back in the day," they were sending out demo tapes, or making friends listen to that tape in their car when they only needed a ride to the laundromat. With the advent of the Internet, that all changed. Your local artist can promote his or her music online, whether bluegrass, death metal, or gospel, and possibly even make a few cents. With this library program, you can help your community's struggling artists put their voice out into the world, not just locally but internationally, in an easy, inexpensive, and effective way.

WHAT PATRONS WILL NEED

- Basic computer skills
- An email account, FB account, or Google+ account
- Preferably some images of their band or themselves, and some sound files

WHAT YOU WILL NEED

- Ability to display an active computer screen (projector monitor or enough room for everyone to gather around)
- An open Internet connection
- Three or more sound files of some sort to load and arrange, or a computer equipped with a microphone.

OUTLINE

1. SoundCloud versus Audiomack or Bandcamp
2. Creating an account
   a. Display name
   b. Unique URL
   c. Real name and location
   d. Your links
   e. Load graphics
3. Loading music
   a. Loading
   b. Recording
4. Albums and playlists
5. Sharing

THE BIG PICTURE

There are many amateur and hobbyist musicians. While SoundCloud can be used to launch a career, it is also a nice way for the full-time accountant, mom and dad, or weekend rocker to share their work. Maybe the soloist at your church, synagogue, or temple would like to share their voice a little farther, or maybe someone in the congregation just likes his or her voice. It can be a nice way to share a child's progress on violin with relatives who cannot make the recitals, or perhaps music teachers would like to showcase the work done by their students. In the end, everyone likes to be heard. As a librarian, you can help them get their voice out there, and as a library you can showcase the talent and arts in your community. The workshop will show patrons how to create an account and load music, but like every class, will allow the patrons to share what they do with each other.

CLASS

SoundCloud versus Audiomack or Bandcamp

The boring part of any presentation is the first 15 minutes of exposition. Make this short, but let patrons know that, although the workshop covers SoundCloud, there are other options. The class is built around SoundCloud because this platform is free, but it does have a tiered pay level, once the user exceeds three hours of music. The second reason to focus on SoundCloud is that it is the most popular platform right now, with 175 million monthly users; of course, by the time you read this, it may not be as popular. Audiomack is growing and may displace SoundCloud, but it is a platform concerned more with tracking your shares and listeners. Bandcamp has a more varied user base, but it also has a lot of features geared toward selling music. Neither of these features will be covered by the program, but let your patrons know about these.

SoundCloud brings you the largest audience by virtue of its popularity. If you really want to know how many people listen to you and share your music, choose Audiomack. If you want to sell t-shirts and albums, choose Bandcamp. The basics of loading music and putting out tracks can be applied to any of these platforms.

CREATING AN ACCOUNT Creating an account in SoundCloud is very similar to signing up for Facebook or any other social media account. The basics you will need are a display name (unlike FB, this can be anything—does not require a real name) and some images for the profile page. Luckily, these can be changed at a later date—even the name, unlike in FB. Logging in will create a generic username; let the patrons use that at first. Navigate to the Profile option on the upper-right side, then choose Edit from the lower-right side of the Profile page. Entering the bio information this way will let patrons see where to change it later. We will be returning to this page later as well.

DISPLAY NAME The first step is to create a name; this will usually be the name of the band. If the patrons do not actually belong to a band, this can be changed later. For patrons who are solo artists or just playing around making music, this can be their personal name. Note that this does not have to be a unique name, so warn your patrons that if they choose the name John Smith, there could be five John Smiths out there making music. This is why a unique URL and location will be important.

UNIQUE URL Patrons should know what URL is, but some patrons may not. The URL is the web address where people can find your music. If the user name is John Smith, the URL needs to be John-Smith_Accordion, or Jane_Smith_Gospel.

It is important to remember that spaces, slashes (/) and periods (.) usually cannot be used in a URL. User names are usually unique identifiers, like with email, and the link will end up being the patron's unique identifier. Changing this unique identifier to something that is not already taken can be challenging. If a patron gets hung up on this step, suggest moving on; he or she can return to this later.

PRO TIP

We have covered this in other programs in this book, but it is always a good idea to craft something, like a bio, in Microsoft Word to copy and paste. Remember: we expect people to know how to copy and paste, but always cover this at least once in a class.

REAL NAME AND LOCATION Providing a real name is not as important, and there is really no need for patrons to enter one unless they want to. Likewise, the location can be left blank. However, this is used later

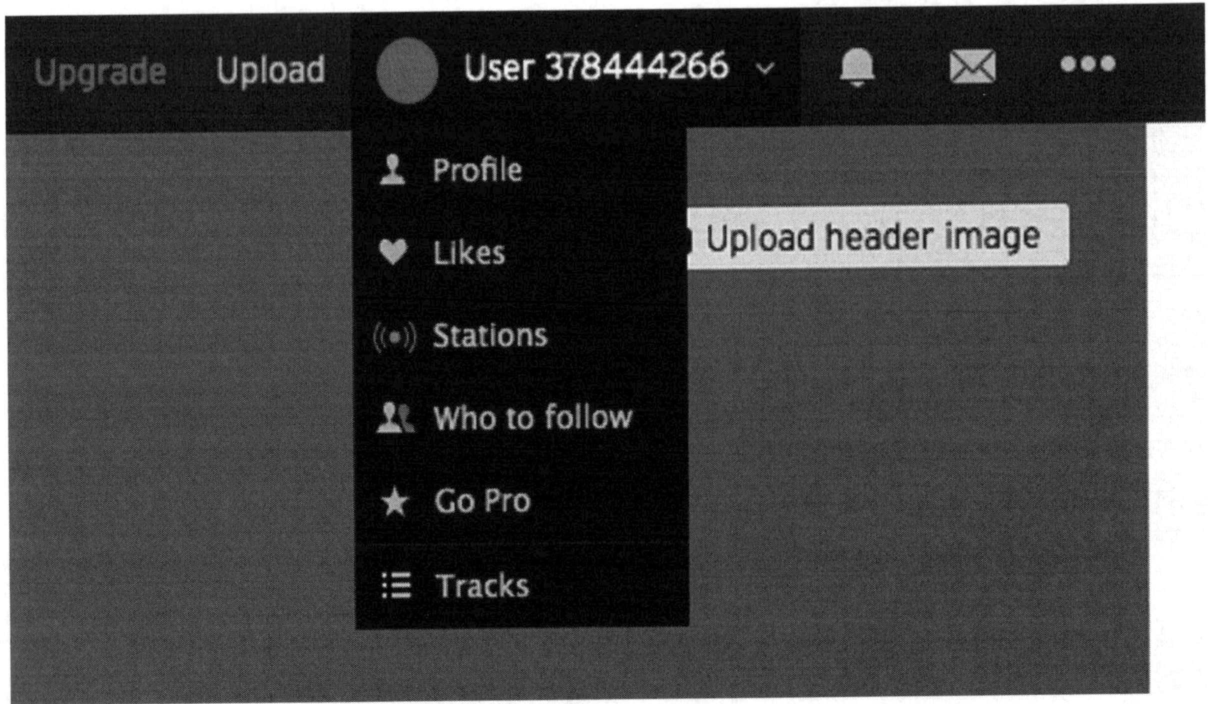

Bandcamp is a social network for bands, allowing bands to share music and be discovered.

for metadata, and can be used to find your patron versus another John Smith. So it may be worth filling out.

If your patrons did not bring in images of their bands or themselves, that is okay. The name, location, and bio are the other elements to fill out. Skip the bio if they do not have one ready.

> **PRO TIP**
>
> **When you talk about making a link, remember that the YouTube workshop in this book (program 3) can be easily changed for a band to share music videos or live footage.**

YOUR LINKS Links are useful for anything—to any videos that might be on YouTube or FB, or to pages for clubs where you play that might sell tickets. There is also a benefit to loading Songkick[1] or BandPage URLs, so that the band can display upcoming show dates. These two sites help bands load tickets and merch (musician shorthand for merchandise). If your patrons are at that point in their music careers, mention that it might be time to find someone to handle their social media.

LOADING IMAGES: HEADER AND PROFILE When you close the Profile interface, you will be back on the main profile page. The image interface is almost identical to that on FB. When you click on the Upload button, you will be asked to load an image. Suggestions for images include:

- At least 800 × 800 for the Profile image (JPEG or PNG)
- At least 2480 × 520 for the Header or Banner image (JPEG or PNG)

Larger images, and images that are the wrong aspect ratio, can be moved around and zoomed in or out, so the larger size is not an issue. A good idea is to bring some of your own images to display for the patrons.

- Zooming is done by clicking and holding the image, then you can drag it to reposition.

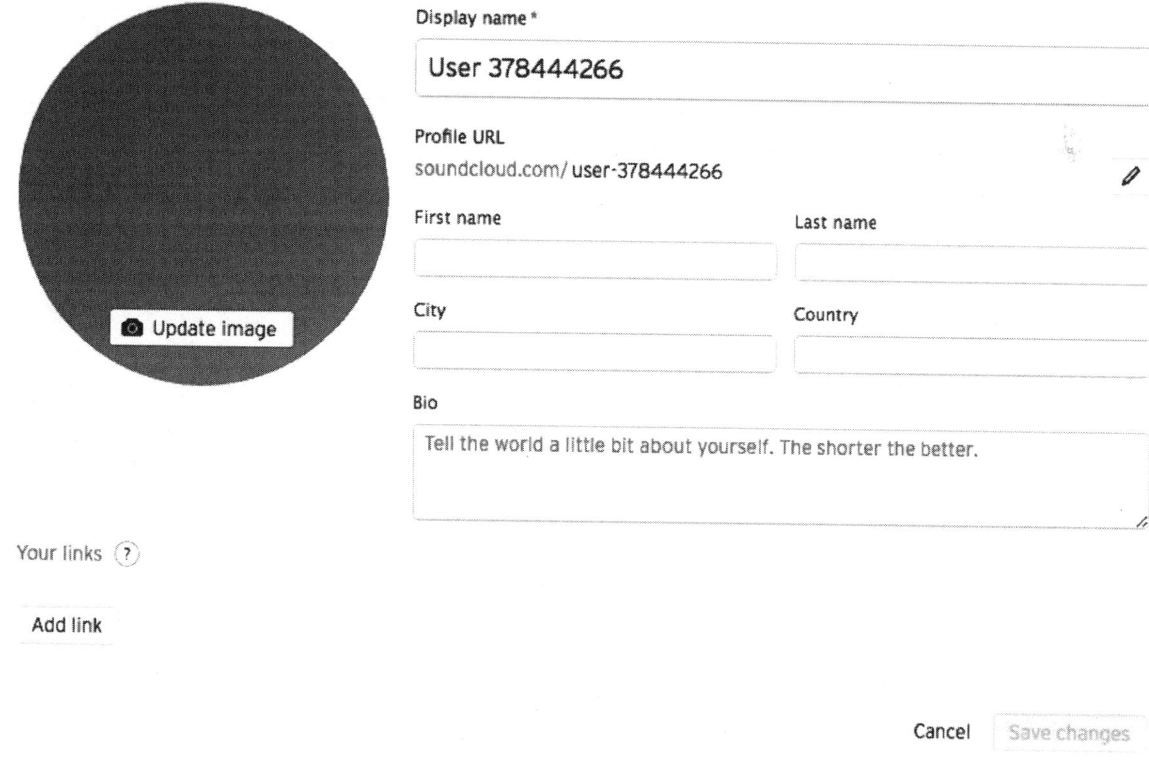

The bio on the Profile in Bandcamp is important to help viewers get a sense of the band.

- If the image is larger than 800 x 800, the small plus (+) and minus (–) can be used to enlarge part of the image to fill the circle.

Loading Music

SoundCloud free usage limits how much music you can load—180 minutes (or 3 hours). SoundCloud will also let you load "live" by recording through your computer. When you load a file, the file can also be made available for download. The original file will be what users can download, so even though SoundCloud creates an MP3 file to play across the web, the original is what will be downloaded.

> **PRO TIP**
>
> **CDs use a 44100 Hz *sample rate*, and 16-bit *sample format*. SoundCloud will accept high-definition formats, usually 32 or 64 bit and larger Hz. However, SoundCloud recompresses everything by saving it again as an MP3, which is why you have a time rather than a size limit. Anything over CD quality can be a waste of time and effort.**

LOADING As mentioned earlier, prerecorded files can be uploaded into SoundCloud. There is a 5-GB size limit; This would be a *huge* sound file. Since this class is focused on musicians, you should have no issues here. If a patron wants to do podcasts, suggest that they try other platforms, although SoundCloud can easily accept podcasts without breaking this size limitation. SoundCloud only accepts certain formats, and you should cover these formats:

- AIFF: the Amiga and, later, Apple format, these are the same files that a CD usually uses and is the standard
- WAVE (WAV): the Microsoft audio file format, also used for CDs on occasion
- FLAC: an open source format, also used for HD sound
- ALAC: Apple's lossless audio codec, up to 32-bit and 384 kHz
- OGG: another open source, low bit rate audio codec, used with open source audio recording
- MP2 and MP3: usually smaller than AIFFs and WAVs but more "lossy"; some believe these do not sound as good
- AAC: Advanced Audio Format, the successor to MP3s, still considered "lossy" but of better sound quality
- AMR: an audio codec that has a smaller dynamic range, made for speech rather than music
- WMA: Windows Media Audio, used by Windows Media Player

Of course, your patrons will not likely need to use all of these. However, as I noted earlier, SoundCloud will recompress everything as an MP3, but the original is available for download. The reason to cover these in class is that if your patrons wish to record and download, you should explain that the best chance for someone to be able to play an audio file is by using the AIFF, WAV, or MP3 formats. FLAC and ALAC formats are for artists concerned about providing the "highest quality" audio, or attracting audiences who want the highest quality. A lot of jazz and classical enthusiasts are consumers of these formats.

RECORDING The recording option is much easier to explain. It is not ideal for an actual band, but you will use this one for the program so that you can walk the class through the next few steps. Select Tracks from the interface; this is the second option located under the header. Clicking this will offer the option to upload a track to view in the center of the screen.

When you click on the text highlighted in blue, it will open a new interface to load or to start a new recording. If you have a microphone handy, record the room saying hello or anything that would take 15–20 seconds to a minute. You can call attention to how the interface is creating a waveform of the audio to fill up the time. When you have finished, press Stop.

The Track Info interface will automatically open. The figure on page 57 shows where you will enter the information for this audio track.

- Title the track anything you like.
- The image should be the same 800 x 800 as the profile image, although it is not necessary.
- You should keep the description short, but because the description does not help with searches, it not entirely necessary.

The next three headings are the most important for making a track "discoverable." If you can, open another browser window onto SoundCloud. Ask your patrons for some of their favorite artists or songs.

Bandcamp's Upload screen for uploading songs and recordings.

> **PRO TIP**
>
> **If you have a media lab, or even if you don't, use a USB microphone to record your patrons. With a USB microphone or media lab, you can show them the resources your library offers. If not, the cost of a microphone is worth the increase in sound quality.**

Use this open window to help patrons understand how Type, Genre, and Tag are used; Refer back to these examples so that they have a better grasp of these searches

- Type is a drop-down menu; use this to find the most appropriate type for your music file. Usually it will be Demo, Recording, Live, or Original.
- Genre is a heading that will be very important. Unfortunately, there is no controlled vocabulary for this. For example, a spiritual or gospel track cannot be put in both genres. This is why we look at other artists; patrons can use an artist who influences them or has a similar sound. Oddly enough, there is a list if you include the tracks in an album. The genre listing can be found at the end of this chapter, so if a patron is making an album, this list can be used for consistency.
- Tags are much more important., Unfortunately, there is no master list of these either. However, it is easy to find a list of trending tags online. All of this can be changed later.

Under Info, you will find settings. These three settings are for the Sharing option, and are fairly self-explanatory.

- Public or Private: You will choose Private, but obviously, patrons will want to change this to Public so their music can be discovered.
- Download or Display Embed Code allow people to download the songs. If users are planning to sell songs, disable these both.
- Make it Personal will allow users to notify others on SoundCloud and connect to social networks when they load a new track.

You can load two or more tracks through the Profile button at the top.

Albums and Playlists

Albums and playlists are not necessary to distribute music on SoundCloud; these are more for marketing. In reality, albums are just playlists marked Album.

If your patron wants to organize their songs into a playlist and an album, the first step will be to create a playlist. Return to the Profile interface from the drop-down menu under user.

When you select Add to Playlist, you will be asked to create a playlist. Again, you will be asked to add

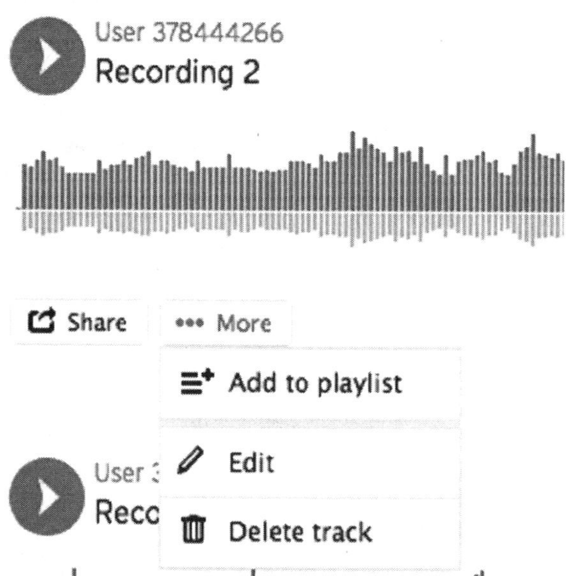

Adding a song to a playlist on Bandcamp will let patrons create an "album" of tracks.

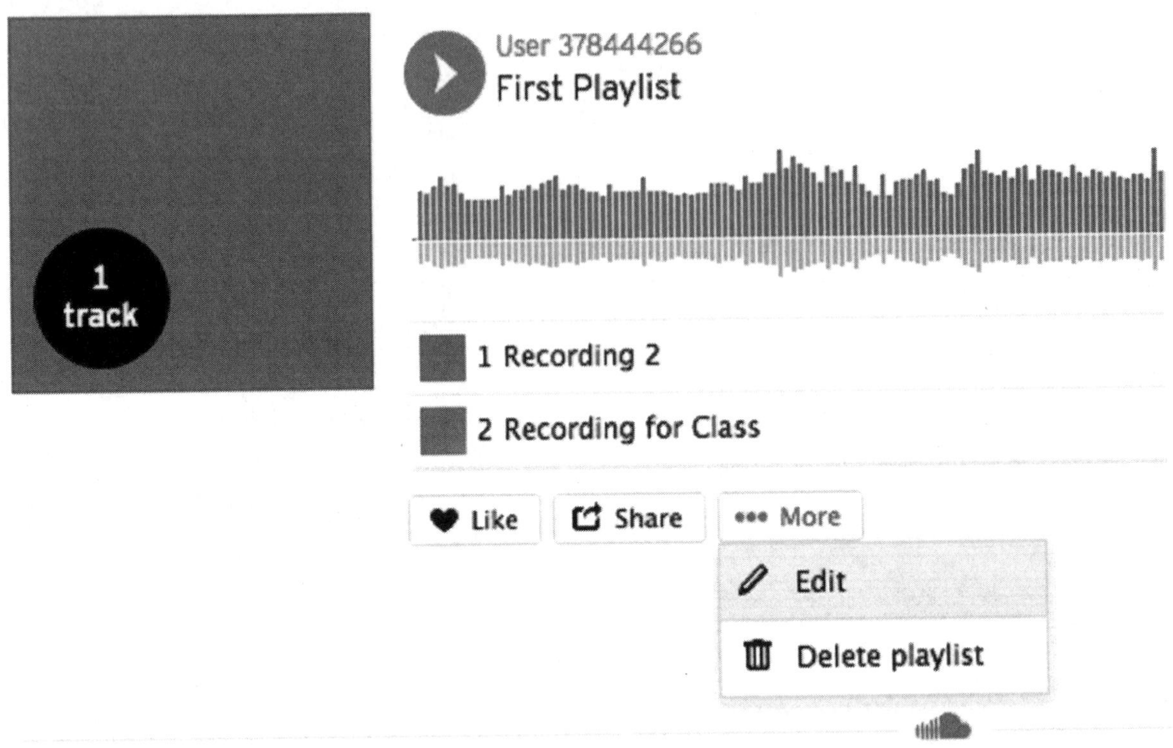

Bandcamp will allow users to modify playlists.

tags; remember how you added tags to the songs, and walk the patrons through this.

After you have created a playlist, you can now create an Album. To do so, go to the Playlist menu item on the Profile page and click on this to open the album interface. Everything your patrons need to do in class will be on the Basic Info screen. They can give their playlist a title separate from the album. Then the Playlist Type needs to be changed to Album. Set a Release Date and go. The release date will announce the album release to anyone following that account.

You will again be asked to specify Genre; there is a drop-down menu of the Genres, and these are listed at the end of this chapter. Tags are like those for the playlists and tracks, but they do NOT replace any tags you put on those earlier. Remember, the description should be kept short.

At this point, your patrons should be able to create and populate a SoundCloud account.

Sharing

Sharing was mentioned in the Track and Album setting directions. However, it is best to cover it again, since the point of SoundCloud is to have the music heard. When the patrons have loaded their tracks, SoundCloud will automatically send the tracks to anyone following them when they make an album. However, if they are taking the class, they are probably not being followed by anyone.

On the Track interface is a Share option under the track; this option is also found under the playlist and the album. Any of these can be shared with Twitter, Facebook, Tumblr, Google+, and Pinterest. These can also be shared with people via email. There is also a link that can be placed on these sites. People who lis-

> PRO TIP
>
> **Set up a library SoundCloud account with your marketing department's permission. When you record the "Hello," have class members say, "We are learning SoundCloud at [your library]." If you have patrons bring in their own recordings, load them and you can put these together in a library playlist, and then link to their SoundCloud accounts at the end of the class. Share this across your social media, and have them share it across theirs.**

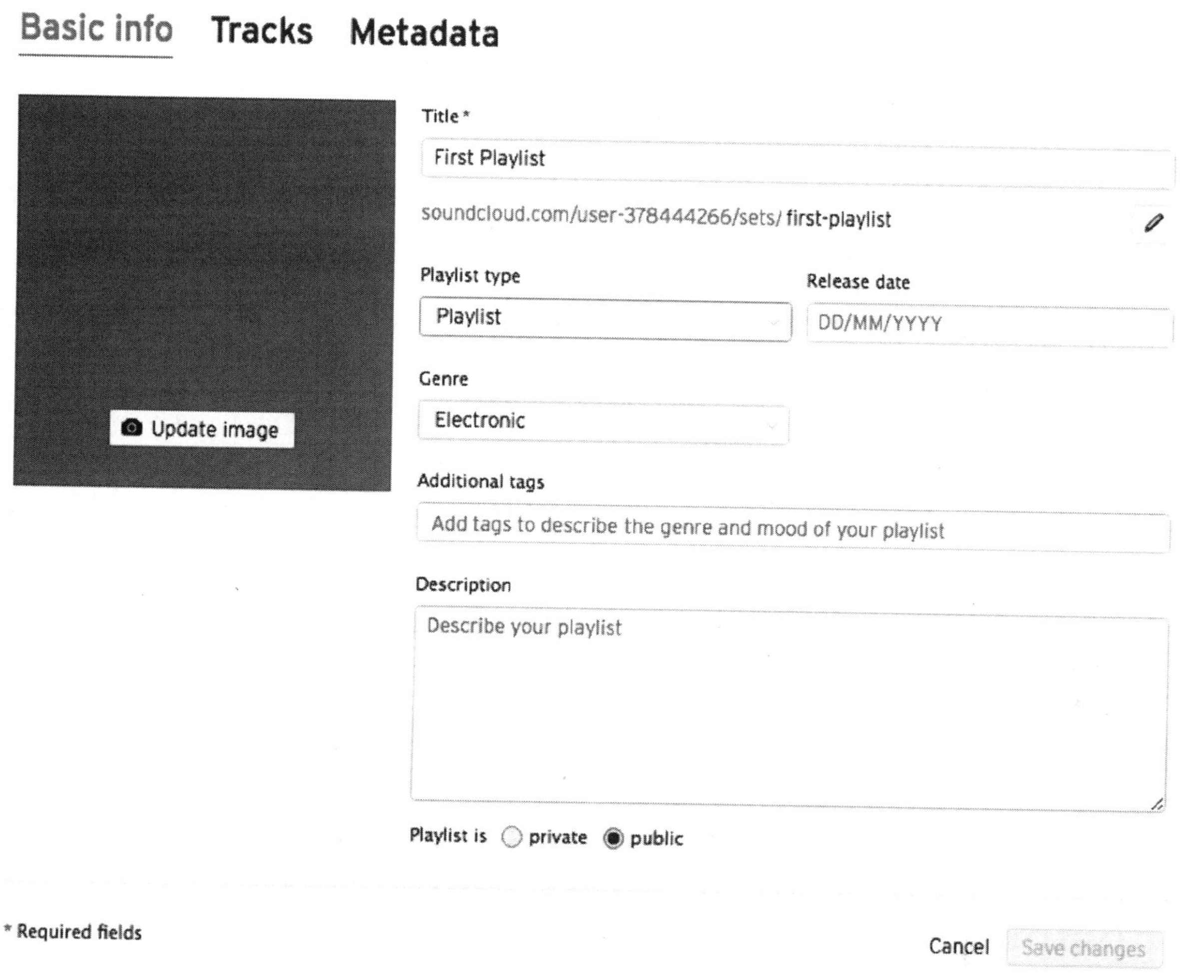

Basic info Tracks Metadata

Title *

First Playlist

soundcloud.com/user-378444266/sets/ first-playlist

Playlist type

Playlist

Release date

DD/MM/YYYY

Genre

Electronic

Update image

Additional tags

Add tags to describe the genre and mood of your playlist

Description

Describe your playlist

Playlist is ○ private ◉ public

* Required fields

Cancel Save changes

Playlists can be released and have artwork, just like albums.

ten to these tracks can join and follow the musician or band. Another way to get followers is to follow others, not unlike Instagram or Twitter. Following someone will often encourage that person to follow you.

HOW THE TOPIC CAME UP AND BECAME A CLASS

The Richmond Public Library was very lucky to host an organization called Girls Rock RVA while I was working there. This group taught young girls and transgendered youth to express themselves by playing rock—loud and hard, as it should be. I was interested in helping the group promote their work at that time. Around the same time, my friend Peggy shared with me her music on SoundCloud via FB, and I discovered that, aside from being an amazing therapist, she is an amazing singer. I thought about how many more unknown talents live in a community, some you may have known for years, and wondered how the library could help these musicians. So I designed this class to help artists get their voices out. The class is designed to be used with a maker space and media lab.

SOUNDCLOUD GENRE LISTING

Alternative Rock
Ambient
Classical
Country
Dance & EDM
Dancehall
Deep House
Disco
Drum & Bass
Dubstep
Electronic
Folk & Singer-Songwriter
Hip-Hop & Rap
House
Indie
Jazz & Blues
Latin
Metal
Piano
Pop
R&B & Soul
Reggae
Reggaeton
Rock
Soundtrack
Techno
Trance
Trap
Triphop
World

NOTE

1. SongKick (http://www.songkick.com/) is a website that allows people to follow bands or shows in their area.

Podcast Your Life

Creating a Theme, Recording, and Sharing a Podcast: Why and Where to Do It

WHY BOTHER?

Podcasting might already seem a little old fashioned to some.

WHAT PATRONS WILL NEED

- Nothing

WHAT YOU WILL NEED

- Ability to display an active computer screen (projector monitor or enough room for everyone to gather around)
- An open Internet connection

OUTLINE

1. Find your thoughts: format
   a. Blog or topical
   b. Personal or panel
2. Find your voice
   a. Find your character:
   b. How to record
   c. What is your microphone?
   d. How do you edit?
3. Find an Audience
   a. Where to host
   b. Where to publish

THE BIG PICTURE

This is another class that is mostly seminar rather than workshop. You will be exposing patrons to podcasting, and asking them the questions that need to be asked before starting, and introducing them to different podcasting tools: microphone, editing software, and platforms for podcasting.

CLASS

Find Your Thoughts: Format

The first step to podcasting is coming up with an idea. Your patrons should feel free to examine any idea, but there are four podcasts that are good examples and that many people enjoy.

- The Art of Charm (http://podbay.fm/show/212382281): This podcast is about personal communication, with a little bit of self-help. It is popular, with over 2 million downloads a month, and has been produced for more than six years.
- Grammar Girls Quick and Dirty Tips for Better Writing (http://podbay.fm/show/173429229): This popular grammar podcast has been on the air for 10 years, and has been ranked as high as second on iTunes.
- The Nerdist (http://podbay.fm/show/355187485): Comedian and TV personality Chris Hardwick started the Nerdist in 2010, and launched the popular Talking Dead podcast and TV show.
- The Moth (http://www.stitcher.com/podcast/the-moth-podcast/e/48916481): The organization dedicated to art of storytelling has been running a weekly podcast since 2009.

Each of these podcasts is a long-running program that has grown from an idea that would not have been thought of as commercial success; these filled a niche and proved successful to the podcasters financially, aesthetically, and personally. Take your patrons to Podbay (http://podbay.fm), then ask about their passions and search for something similar.

BLOG OR TOPICAL The next question in preparing a podcast is: What is your format, blog or topical? A blog podcast is for a single issue or concern, like Grammar Girl, or the Art of Charm. Does the patron blog now? Has he or she thought of turning the blog into a podcast? A topical podcast is more like a news show. The Nerdist is topical, although every topic has to do with "nerd" culture.

Deciding on a format will help patrons understand what their needs will be when they start to generate podcasts, how to describe the podcast and, more importantly, how to record it.

PERSONAL OR PANEL Ask your patrons, "Who will talk in your podcast?" Will it be the patron and a cohost discussing topics, or will there be a host that will invite people to speak? Or will the podcast have a panel each time? Art of Charm is a host and cohost team, and they interview people. Grammar Girl is a host with a topic. The Nerdist has a panel discussing topics. The Moth has a guest each week.

The easiest way to do a podcast is to have one person talking; a cohost can help make it livelier, and a panel even livelier still. But the more people involved, the greater the time and equipment. Ask your patrons:

- What format do they want?
- Do they have a person with whom to talk about the topic?
- If they would like to have a guest or a panel, could they find enough people to ask?

Discuss the host format:

- Pros: easy, less equipment, less organizing for recording
- Cons: the host's character and personality need to carry the show, more planning for topics (host must fill the half-hour)

Discuss the host/cohost/panel formats:

- Pros: livelier, can explore a topic from separate points of view more effectively; panels can have rotating members.
- Cons: more equipment, more planning to get everyone at same place and same time, more editing (easier to go overtime)

Discuss the interview format:

- Pros: more varied from week to week, different points of view
- Cons: more organizing for recording (need to schedule guests), more planning for interview, more equipment, probably more editing (guests can go overtime)

Ask your patrons: What do they think they could manage in their time? Do they need a panel? Are they prepared to talk for a half-hour at least by themselves? If they want guests or a panel, can they plan three weeks in advance (at least) for the topic?

Find Your Voice: Recording

You have discussed with your patrons the format; now the method can be addressed. The bare minimum for a podcast is a microphone and a computer that can record audio. It really is that easy. However, that easy is not usually that good.

HOW TO RECORD: SETTING UP A ROOM FOR PODCASTING A room for podcasting needs to be *quiet*. This means it needs to be isolated from traffic noise, street noise, other voices, and a lot of noises we do not notice very often. Ask the patrons to be quiet for a second. do you hear the air conditioning going in the room you are in? A microphone will pick that up. Do you hear traffic running by, or is there a fan? A microphone will pick those up as well.

To record, a room will also need to have the audio controlled. That means no fans, air conditioning turned off in the room (or at least not noisy), and you will need to avoid sound reflection. Sound reflection is sound (your voice, etc.,) that bounces off the wall; it is also called echo.

An easy way to demonstrate this is with a cell phone, or a computer and microphone. If you can play your cell phone loud enough, use the voice recorder on your phone to record yourself speaking, then put it on speakerphone and record your voice. Play both back for the patrons. The hollow echoing is sound reflection. The patrons can fight this by using anything that absorbs sound. Some inexpensive options:

- Use a closet—the clothes are sound-muffling.
- Surround yourself with mattresses; as ridiculous as this sounds, it works.
- Hang heavy curtains around the sides of the room. Sheets would not work because they are too light; better put those on your mattress.
- Carpet—using carpet remnants or samples is an old method to create cheap sound booths.

Of course, not all of these will work; for example, a panel show would be hard to surround with mattresses, and a guest to interview may be suspicious if you ask them to step into your closet.

WHAT IS YOUR MICROPHONE? You can now move on to discussing microphones with your patrons. If your library has a microphone, or different types of microphones, it is a good idea to let the patrons handle these.

PRO TIP

Does your library have media lab? Do you have microphones or a sound booth? Now is the time to promote these resources in the class.

You may not have all the types I will discuss, but you can search them easily enough. The preferred way of recording for podcasters is on a studio or USB condenser microphone. The Yeti is the bestseller on Amazon; it is very popular with podcasters and video bloggers. It is also about $100 at the time of this writing.

There are basically two types of microphones: condenser and dynamic. Condensers are more sensitive and require power. In general, condenser microphones are also more expensive. Dynamic mics are cheaper, more forgiving of ambient sound if you do not have a sound booth, and require no power. Both can be found with analog and USB connections as well. If you use an analog connector, it must be plugged into the computer's specific mic jack. If it is an analog condenser, it will need a mixer to provide it power. For this reason, most podcasters use USB microphones. These can be connected to a computer without a mixer.

However, some podcasters like a headset, like those used for gaming. If the patrons are just starting out, then this is usually a cheaper way. It would not work for panel or interview format, and either of those would likely require more than one mic, which should be a consideration of the patrons.

A USB microphone appropriate for podcasting. *Katie Chan (own work) [CC BY-SA 3.0 (http://creativecommons.org/licenses/by-sa/3.0)], via Wikimedia Commons*

HOW DO YOU EDIT? The final consideration is editing. Editing is most often done in a stand-alone program like Audacity, which is the software patrons will use to record their podcast and then upload their files to the distribution sites. Of course it is possible to not edit, to record a podcast in one long take. Indeed, a program like SoundCloud or Bandcamp will let you record straight to the site without any editing. It is rarely the best solution.

For this shorter program, it will be enough to explain why and what they can use to edit. Reasons to edit include:

- Multiple takes: editing can correct mistakes, whether these are mispronunciations or unexpected interruptions (like a dropped mic, or a phone call)
- Break a podcast into multiple sessions: If your podcast is 30 minutes long, you can record in 15- or 10- or 5-minute sessions. It can be quite a strain on the voice to talk for half an hour straight.
- Record more than you need and edit down: Especially in interview situations, you might find that the interview ran long. Afterward, you can choose which parts make the best podcast.

What software to use?

- Audacity is free software that can be found easily online. It can edit as well as correct audio and apply filters. Audacity is very popular with podcasters.
- MP3DirectCut is also free, and is much more basic. It can be used to trim down takes and stitch them together, more easily than with Audacity.
- Windows Media Player on PCs, or GarageBand on MACs: every computer with windows or MacOS has a program for recording audio. Garageband is a much more refined and sophisticated program than Windows Media Player, but is geared more toward music than voiceovers.

Including a tutorial on editing is up to you as the instructor. I think editing should be a class in itself, and it is definitely an advanced class rather than an intermediate class like others in this book. If you have the ability and interest, you can show patrons some

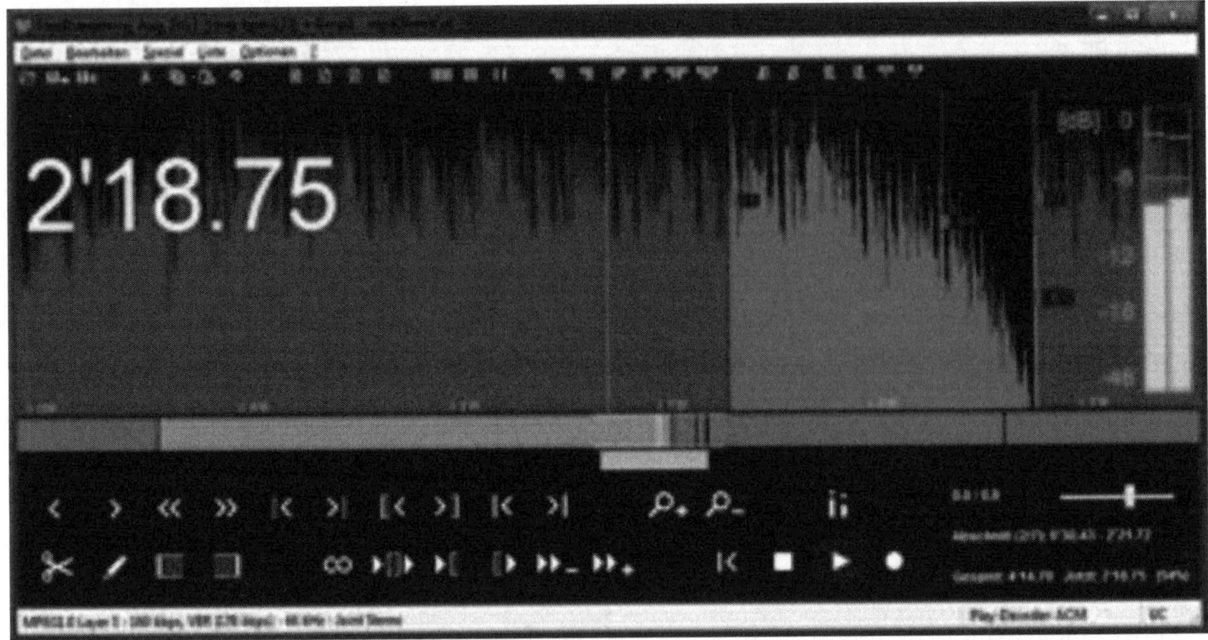

Audacity is a great editing program for audio, if your patron is serious about their recordings. ***http://www.mpesch3.de1.cc/mp3dc.html***

editing programs. However, this is a risky endeavor since they are likely to want to see them used.

Find an Audience

The final step is to show the patrons how to find an audience and where to host their podcasts. You will address hosting first. Something to understand is that a podcast must be stored on a server somewhere; if your patrons have a web page or blog, it probably won't be a good idea to host the podcast there. Audio files are big files—not as big as video, but big enough so that a normal web hosting site is not necessarily capable of hosting a podcast and allowing people listen to it in an acceptable way.

If the patrons have a problem understanding this, ask them if they have ever tried to watch a streaming video and waited while the video was buffering. The buffering spinner is a very frustrating experience, but it lets us know that the server cannot load the file. If patrons do not want to have a spinner . . . they will need a good host.

Some of the better hosts are:

- Archive.org: one of the older solutions on the web, this site will host a podcast for free. Also worth mentioning is that it has no size limit and gives multiple embed options. The downside is that it is slower than other options. Also of interest, this site hosts the Wayback Machine.
- Podbean: this is a free hosting option that limits your hosting to 30 MB files. That can be a sizeable audio file.
- SoundCloud: the website most known for music is another free option. The downside is that it limits you to 120 minutes of audio, so that would be only four podcasts. The upside is that SoundCloud's interface will allow patrons to record directly to the site.
- libsyn is a paid podcasting site, and one of the older ones. It is only $5 a month, but will be fast, with no size limitation. It also has syndication and publishing tools.

Once you have a host, you have to publish a podcast. This is where people will be looking for your podcast. When we were identifying podcasts earlier in the class, you saw some of the options. Here are a few of the major ones:

- iTunes: the iTunes store is where podcasting first became a commercial success
- Google Play: basically, iTunes for android devices, but the major outlet for podcasts on non-Apple products
- Stitcher: a searchable index of over 65,000 radio shows and podcasts, available on PC and Mac computers, and smart devices.

HOW THE TOPIC CAME UP AND BECAME A CLASS

I asked a friend of mine, Carl Hamm, to run a class on podcasting. He had run a podcast of his radio show, *If Music Could Talk*, for years on the independent radio station WRIR. He was very nice to agree to do this. He was not able to cover as much as he wanted, I noticed, because he was teaching the editing on Audacity. I took note of where he bogged down, along with the fact that the audience was unfamiliar with the generalities of podcasts. While some of them had heard podcasts, they were not really familiar with the process. This class is a response to patrons wanting to know the basic processes and sites to start their own podcast.

Part III

PROGRAMS FOR PROFESSIONAL LIFE

These classes are designed to help your patrons grow a business. An independent businessperson does not have the resources of larger organizations. Libraries can bridge that divide by showing patrons some free resources to help start, or grow, a small business. The classes are for business ranging from a small sideline job, to a brick-and-mortar location. In any case, the library can help patrons learn the basics of what their competitors are doing to be more successful.

Searching for Jobs, Beyond Monster and Classifieds

Indeed and Special Job Boards

WHY BOTHER?

Job searching is always a need in any community, especially in economically distressed areas. Or, if you're in an affluent neighborhood, there are always students, homemakers, and seniors who may be looking for part-time work. For those people this would be a helpful program. It is not about finding a job, but finding the right job, and how to make a more targeted attempt at employment.

People know about using sites like Monster and Indeed for broad searches for work. For some people, job hunting is easily done through work-related boards, like the American Library Association's board or your state's Library Association boards. If your patrons are not looking with such a narrow focus, there is a middle ground too. Patrons can use set up alerts for jobs that meet their needs on a site called Indeed. There are also sites for searching for work based not on industry, but on work conditions, like freelance or "flex" work. We cannot cover those interfaces in detail, but you can help patrons become aware of the options.

WHAT PATRONS WILL NEED

- Basic computer skills
- An email account
- A resume in digital format
- An idea of what kind of work they are looking for

WHAT YOU WILL NEED

- An open Internet connection
- A premade LinkedIn account
- Ability to display an active computer screen (projector monitor, or enough room for everyone to gather around)

OUTLINE

1. Creating an account on Indeed
2. Helping Patrons set up their search parameters
   a. Age
   b. Location
   c. Salary estimate
   d. Show jobs from
   e. Job type
   f. Company
3. Meta tags and search parameters
   a. With these words in title
   b. With none of these words in title
   c. Refining a search or broadening it
4. Specialized job boards

THE BIG PICTURE

The fun part of this class for your patrons is that they get to interact with another person and solidify what they are looking for in a job. A large part of the class is really just a chance for the patron to focus on what he or she is looking for and, by having another patron to talk to, refine what kind of job to look for. Patrons will think through search terms and run them past one another before starting a search. For you, the fun part of this class is that it is really an information literacy and Boolean operator class, disguised as job searching. You are walking though one interface, in this case Indeed, but either Monster and Indeed can be used. Both websites will let you use Boolean logic

PRO TIP

In computer classes, you are always asking patrons to create a password. Password security is a huge issue, but a more problematic issue is patrons remembering their passwords.

I prefer to use a formula:

Mother's name + year they graduated + a special character that corresponds to holding the shift key while pressing the first number of the month they were born. For example, for a patron born in October, the 10th month means using first the number 1, shift + 1 equals !)

The trade-off in security for being able to remember a password is worth the effort.

in a search. You are really walking patrons through an advanced search to show them how Boolean operators work. They can then apply Boolean logic to refine their own search.

CLASS

Creating an Account on Indeed

Setting up an Indeed account is easy. Ask the patrons to navigate to Indeed https://www.indeed.com/). In the upper-right corner of the Indeed home page is a button to sign in. Patrons will need to use their email account and create a password. Patrons have the option to sign in with their FB profile, but I suggest you discourage this, as they do not want to broadcast their job search to coworkers.

Helping Patrons Set Up Search Parameters

After the patron has created an account, an Advanced Job Search box will open in Indeed. I find it easier to work from the bottom of this search interface, as the questions are more specific and easier to answer going up because the interface moves from the general to the specific.

Before patrons fill out the search, you want to make sure they know what they are looking for. Patrons should bring their resumes. You can pair up patrons. Have them ask each other questions, so that the person listening to the search description understands what their partner is looking for. While one patron is talking, the other patron writes down the terms they hear. They switch at the end, and show and share the terms. It may not provide useful results, but it usually does and, more importantly, the interaction helps the patrons focus on what they are looking for by having to articulate their search. Of course, if they are not comfortable sharing in a class, do not make them.

If a patron says, "I want to work at an easy job during the day," ask them what is easy. If the response is, "I like talking to people and clothes," we have search terms such as:

- Part time
- First shift
- Retail
- Customer service
- Fashion

Treat this as a reference question; you will need to understand the key words used by job boards. Understanding key words is problematic, because there is

Advanced Job Search

Find Jobs

With **all** of these words	
With the **exact phrase**	
With **at least one** of these words	
With **none** of these words	
With these words in the **title**	
From this **company**	
Show jobs of type	All job types
Show jobs from	All web sites
	☐ Exclude staffing agencies
Salary estimate	per year $50,000 or $40K-$90K

Where and When

Location within 25 miles of | Burke, VA | (city, state, or zip)

Age - Jobs published | anytime

Display 10 results per page,sorted by relevance | Find Jobs

The Advanced Search for job hunting on Indeed

no controlled vocabulary for job searching. You may have to try several synonyms or different approaches. Explain to the patrons that when they try a search, it is best to pay attention to the terms used by classified ads, as they may see something that describes their work in language they do not generally use.

When the patrons have written down their search terms, have each pair take a minute or two to choose the terms they want, and add any terms they think the other patron has missed. Now you can start to walk the patrons through Indeed's Advanced Job Search interface.

AGE (OF PUBLISHED JOBS) From the bottom of the interface up, skipping the number of alerts to show, we start with Age. It describes the age of the advertisements, just to be clear. If it is the first time patrons have set up a search, the default, Anytime, is fine. With a search they are returning to, it will be less likely to return useful results because previously viewed jobs will be listed.

The drop-down menu has five other options:

- Within 15 days
- Within 7 days
- Within 3 days
- Since yesterday
- Since my last visit

I think the most flexible would be "Since my last visit." As with most things, the option can be changed.

LOCATION Next is Location; patrons must decide how far they are willing to travel. Also, tell them to use the most specific term they can. If you live in a large city with multiple zip codes, use your zip code; if you're in a rural area, use the city name.

SALARY ESTIMATE My suggestion is to leave that blank, unless this is the primary reason they are looking for a job. You will be able to refine this from results page. You may notice this is a per-year interface, so $20,000 per year salary is a $10 per hour job. However, because the *employer* fills in this field, so there is no control or guarantee of consistency. It is fair to warn the patrons that they need to be careful. An ad may state $20,000 a year, but that means *if* you worked full time; the actual job could be $10 an hour, 15 hours a week. Your classes may have homemakers or retirees or students, and a per year salary search is not ideal if you are working with people looking for part-time or freelance work. A per our wage can be used as a key term: $12.

SHOW JOBS FROM There are three choices here: All websites, Job boards, Company sites. Dealing with all websites is probably the best option. When you encounter a patron looking for a specific company or agency, they can specify that. This is not very common, since Indeed's appeal is that it is an aggregator versus a job board, so that it searches other job boards and websites. You can take this opportunity to explain to the patrons what an aggregator is, and since classifieds in local newspapers are no longer the predominant way to advertise, a job search needs to be across multiple sites to be effective at all. The one useful part of this option is the staffing agency exclusion. If patrons are NOT looking for temporary work, it is a good idea to remove this option, and since the class is geared toward the *right* job, excluding agencies would be best for the patrons who attend.

JOB TYPE The options are:

- Internship
- Commission
- Contract
- Temporary
- Part time
- Full time

Tell your patrons that they should choose an option *only* if they want a specific type. Take Contract, for instance. Unfortunately, this interface only allows a *single* selection, so you cannot use it to create an *exclusion* interface, (the option of choosing all that apply). For example, to find a permanent job, you cannot remove Internships, Temporary, and Contract work, but must choose the permanent options individually. Likewise, you will have to choose Full time, or Part time in two separate searches. Or, if you want temporary or contract work, you would create two separate searches with those keywords.

COMPANY Searching for a specific company is especially useful if there is a large company in your area that has appeal. Indeed would only be useful if the employer website doesn't create alerts itself. If someone is looking for work from a specific company, suggest they make sure the corporate website does not create alerts.

Key Words, Terms, and Search Parameters

At this point you will ask the patrons to review the key words or terms they came up with when working with the other patron. Has the key word been covered by the interface so far? Do they want a job at a specific company, or do they want a specific type of work? The remaining terms on their list will be what they will use as a guide for the rest of the search. Explain to the patrons that they are basically doing a key word search. The key words are drawn from the text of the ad or the title. It is important to point out that these terms are *not* controlled, so if the term they are using is carpenter, there may be an ad for cabinetmaker that will not show up as a search result.

> **PRO TIP**
>
> **Boolean logic and Venn diagrams may seem a bit excessive for workshop, but I feel like they are worthwhile. I understand that this would seem like a "lecture," but it is easier for some people to grasp ideas from a visual aid.**

As librarians, we know how to do searches, but you must think like a job hunter. They are not used to thinking about what they do, or how they define it. You also need to remember that your patrons might not know the specific language that employers are using. So, really, this search process is making them aware of the "possible terms" they could use in their search and creating a Boolean operator from that.

Remember, we are working from the bottom up.

WITH THESE WORDS IN TITLE The first parameter is terms in the job ad title only. Again, these are the terms that apply to the field of work or to a specific title for a position. Patrons need to think about how the terms are used in their field, to separate the broad descriptive terms from the specific ones. For a title, the term needs to be specific in regard to type of work or position, but broad in terms of the field. Take the word Office; is it office work a patron is looking for? That would be good for a title, but not a key word. Office is a broad term for white-collar work, but it is specific to an *office manager*. You would not use this in a key word search, because you may end up with "veterinary assistant to work in our office," but you might use it in a title search to bring up results for a manager position in an office.

Another example would be the term Plumbing. Perhaps a patron would be willing to work in a plumbing store, or be an apartment superintendent. He or she should not use Plumbing in the title search, since this will bring those options forward, versus using Plumbing as a key word or exact phrase. Or, plumbing sales could be a very specific type of sales, but Sales or Salesperson would be the broader term to use in the Title search.

WITH NONE OF THESE WORDS IN THE TITLE Ask the patrons about the limitations they place on their job hunt. Some good terms to think about excluding from a title are: Travel, Commission, Canvasing, Temporary, Internship, Unpaid Internship. Often these terms will show up in a title as well as in a key word search.

> **PRO TIP**
>
> **It is worthwhile to keep a list of bad search terms if you run this program more than once. Collect them from the searches you run with patrons. Put them on the board, and discuss what they mean in context, like Canvasing indicating a job involving a lot of walking.**

At this point you want them to search. Look at the number of returns they get. You may need to get more specific, especially as that is the goal of this class to refine results.

KEY WORDS The remaining three options in the interface apply to the main body text of the advertisements. Use these search options to show the patrons how to refine the search based on their key words for their *skills*, like Microsoft Office knowledge, or carpentry skills. I consider skills to be the most useful way to refine the search, but this will depend on what they want; a patron may be looking for travel, or a job in a school. When searching the body of an ad, more specific text can be used. The three fields are:

- With at least one of these words: key words used in this box will function as if the Boolean operator OR was used
- With None of these words in the title: key words used in this text box will act as if the Boolean operator NOT was used
- With the exact phrase: key words used in this text box will react as if quotation marks ("exact term") were used
- With all of these words: key words used in this text box will act as if the Boolean operator AND was used

Make note of any terms you use in these fields. You can have the patrons try different search options in turn. Several searches may be necessary if the terms are too

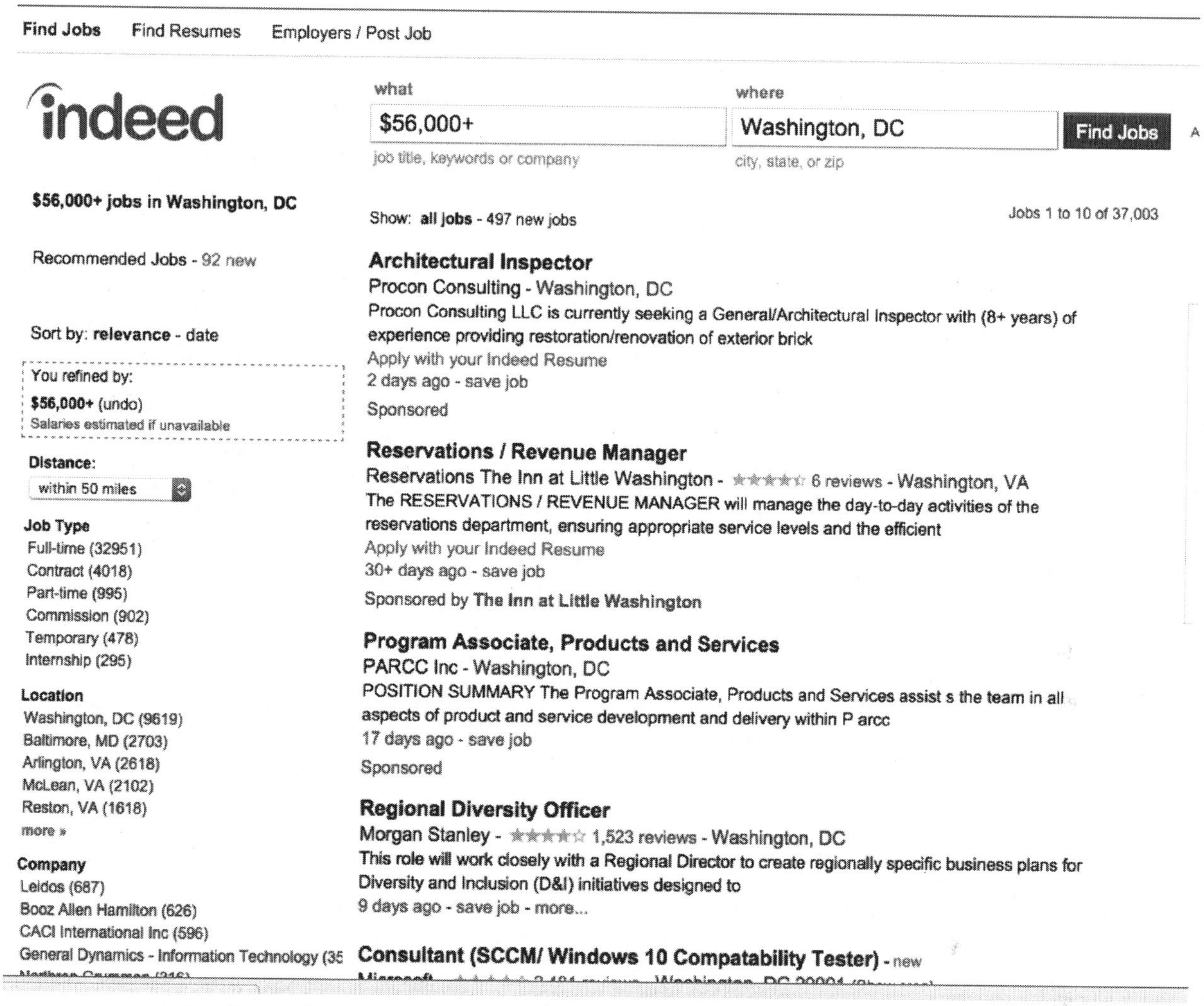

Find Jobs Find Resumes Employers / Post Job

indeed

what: $56,000+ (job title, keywords or company)
where: Washington, DC (city, state, or zip)
Find Jobs

$56,000+ jobs in Washington, DC

Recommended Jobs - 92 new

Sort by: **relevance** - date

You refined by:
$56,000+ (undo)
Salaries estimated if unavailable

Distance: within 50 miles

Job Type
Full-time (32951)
Contract (4018)
Part-time (995)
Commission (902)
Temporary (478)
Internship (295)

Location
Washington, DC (9619)
Baltimore, MD (2703)
Arlington, VA (2618)
McLean, VA (2102)
Reston, VA (1618)
more »

Company
Leidos (687)
Booz Allen Hamilton (626)
CACI International Inc (596)
General Dynamics - Information Technology (35

Show: **all jobs** - 497 new jobs

Jobs 1 to 10 of 37,003

Architectural Inspector
Procon Consulting - Washington, DC
Procon Consulting LLC is currently seeking a General/Architectural Inspector with (8+ years) of experience providing restoration/renovation of exterior brick
Apply with your Indeed Resume
2 days ago - save job
Sponsored

Reservations / Revenue Manager
Reservations The Inn at Little Washington - 6 reviews - Washington, VA
The RESERVATIONS / REVENUE MANAGER will manage the day-to-day activities of the reservations department, ensuring appropriate service levels and the efficient
Apply with your Indeed Resume
30+ days ago - save job
Sponsored by **The Inn at Little Washington**

Program Associate, Products and Services
PARCC Inc - Washington, DC
POSITION SUMMARY The Program Associate, Products and Services assist s the team in all aspects of product and service development and delivery within P arcc
17 days ago - save job
Sponsored

Regional Diversity Officer
Morgan Stanley - 1,523 reviews - Washington, DC
This role will work closely with a Regional Director to create regionally specific business plans for Diversity and Inclusion (D&I) initiatives designed to
9 days ago - save job - more...

Consultant (SCCM/ Windows 10 Compatability Tester) - new

Searches can be modified in Indeed after submitting options from the menu on the left.

narrow. Repeat searches have value because of the lack of controlled vocabulary I have noted before. This will require filling out the interface several times, but that is why you have the terms written down. Explain to the patrons to make notes on which ones have better returns. Sometimes too few returns will come up when they fill in more than one refinement, like Microsoft Word and Education, or Plumbing and Wholesale. It may be that their terms are too narrow, or that the field they are looking in is too small. It might be worthwhile to compare which terms result in jobs closer to what they desire. When patrons have all their terms in, make sure to check them against what they have written down.

REFINING THE SEARCH, OR BROADENING IT When patrons submit their search, they will see that search reflected in the left-hand column of the page showing their results. Patrons will have a choice of making a new search, or they can broaden or refine the search with the interface on the left side of the search returns. The problem with the advanced search is that it does not Save as an option. If a patron signs into Indeed and makes a simple search by location and keyword, it will save the search, and the next time the patron logs in, the search is available in the left-hand column. This is why you will have the patron write down their key words for an advanced search.

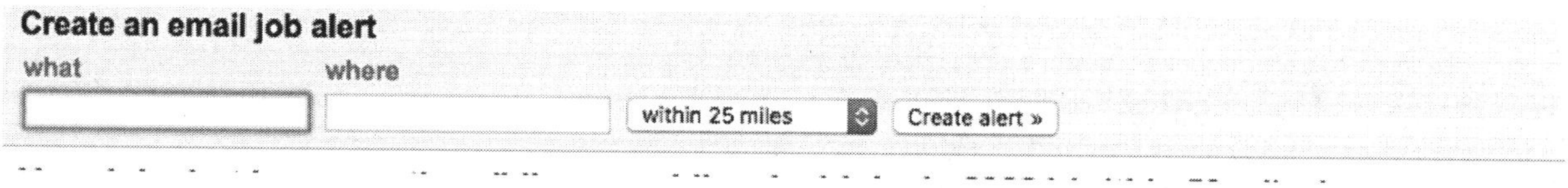

Create an email job alert
what where within 25 miles Create alert »

Patrons unable to or unwilling to commute can limit the distance for a job search.

At this point, your patrons have the ability to make a refined search with Indeed. One other feature of Indeed is the ability to set alerts. The site does not allow you to make advanced search alerts, which would be a fantastic tool. However, making alerts with the simplified search will allow patrons to be notified whenever a job meeting their criteria is listed.

Ask the patrons to again refer to their notes and see which search terms they used for the Boolean fields in the Advanced Job Search interface. For example, a patron uses key terms with AND between them. A quick reminder: Boolean logic requires you keep the terms NOT, AND, OR, & " " in all caps. It is a good way to refine search alerts.

Specialized Job Boards

There are also more specific job boards available for specific careers. We can cover these and how they can be used to drill down patron searches; however, many are for-pay sites or are more focused, so it is not really feasible to run a class on these sites. I suggest these as more of a way to start conversations and enhance a "finding the right job" class. If you have a small enough group of patrons, you can log on to some of these sites and perhaps conduct a job search on one. For instance, while we know there is an ALA job board, if would be unlikely that you would have a librarian in the class, so planning beyond the basics will not help.

> **PRO TIP**
>
> **Many libraries keep a list of job search sites on their web page. However, updating that page can be daunting, and the first category of freelance and special boards is especially hard to keep up. With specialized boards appearing and disappearing all the time based on their popularity, an online resource might not be feasible. For the same reason, when you run this class, a handout or web resource may not be possible. However, you can keep a list and bookmark the sites you visit, as they may come up again.**

FREELANCE BOARDS AND SPECIAL BOARDS More people work from home, or work side jobs. Traditionally, that sort of work is found through word of mouth. Now, however, the Internet makes it possible for people to launch their search without a great number of contacts. The problem with any sort of work-from-home situation or freelance work is *getting paid*. The websites that I choose do vet their jobs, and although many are for-pay sites, these may be worth the cost.

- Flexjobs: *Forbes* magazine rated this site as the "best overall site for homeworkers."[1] I would suggest this for people who want to work from home. It has a wide variety of freelance, telecommuting, and temporary work. It costs $15 a month. It is however, fairly easy to use.
- UpWork.com: freelance opportunities, for which the website handles billing and payment.
- Outsource.com: a wider variety of jobs. It has a simple interface but a more professional level of work.
- SalesGravy.com: site for commission and sales jobs.

GOVERNMENT JOBS

- USAjobs.gov: the federal government's website for government jobs
- Governmentjobs.com: a website used by state, county, and local governments to post open positions

Often, your city, county, and state will have their own special job sites. It is useful to point this out to your patrons.

LINKEDIN The problem many people have is that a "perfect job" is not going to be on Indeed. Advertised jobs are still just cattle calls for people. In the past, the only way to get a good job was by networking—knowing the people in your field, and those people knowing you and what you can do, or knowing that you have that "something" that makes them want to work with you. Unlike job searching in the past, where the only way to plug into a network of employees was by running into them, there are now websites for various industries. LinkedIn is the most broadly popular, and will even allow job searching from it. The real benefit to using LinkedIn, however, is that is it can also serve as reference and resume to employers who search through that site.

HOW THE TOPIC CAME UP AND BECAME A CLASS

Resume classes are pretty common, but I noticed that I spent a lot of time working with people on finding a job. After a certain point there were some common tricks I used to find jobs, like going to Indeed, and referring patrons to government sites on our library's web page. I do not suggest that this class can replace working with patrons one-on-one, but a class does free up a *lot* of time. The class is a way to collect some best practices into one event, so, hopefully, you can guide people and reduce demands on the time of your staff.

NOTE

1. Nancy Collamer, "10 More Great Sites to Find Gigs and Part-Time Work," *Forbes*, June 13, 2016. https://www.forbes.com/sites/nextavenue/2016/06/13/10-more-great-sites-to-find-gigs-and-part-time-work/#721a26a79d53.

Share, Don't Steal

How to Safely Get Images, Sounds, and Video Off the Web

WHY BOTHER?

At some point a patron will need help downloading an image off the Internet. If you're just grabbing an image for a school report or for a joke to a friend, it is not a big deal to download whatever you want. However, as a librarian, you know that approach should not be used for something for print, on a blog, or for a commercial purpose. Even for a community flyer, or for any kind of web use, patrons could open themselves up to a potential lawsuit. As librarians, we understand the purpose of copyright, but rather than just tell patrons that copyright infringement is not the right thing to do, we can instead offer them an opportunity to discover how to properly access and use copyrighted material.

WHAT PATRONS WILL NEED

- Basic computer skills
- Ability to download software from the web

WHAT YOU WILL NEED

- An idea about what patrons want to look for
- An open Internet connection

OUTLINE

1. Grabbing off Google
    a. How to search for images
        i. Size constraints
        ii. Types of images
        iii. Refining by license
2. Copyright Primer
    a. Fair use
    b. What does CC mean?
3. Cheap and Free Images, Sounds, Video, and Fonts
    a. Sites for free images
    b. Sites for free sounds
    c. Free Fonts

THE BIG PICTURE

This class shows patrons how to acquire images from the Internet that can be used for anything, including commercial purposes. It will also show them a wide range of available resources, not only images but video, audio, and fonts. The class is designed to help patrons not only get the right kind of picture, but pictures they have the right to use. It could also introduce Creative Commons (CC) to people who have never heard of it.

CLASS

Grabbing off Google

Why teach Google for searching? Besides its popularity, Google is a great search engine. Bing and Yahoo are great search engines, too, But Google was the first to introduce the idea of image searches, so it has the benefit of being the more mature interface for image searching. You can try other engines, and I suggest these in class, but a good way to get people introduced to these ideas is Google.

How to Search for Images

You start the search for an image the same way you do for websites—from the Google box. For example, if you ask the patrons to search "Library book":

1. Type "Library book" in the search bar.
2. At first you will see the web results, with a menu across the bottom of the header. Have the patrons select Images; the page will return only images.
3. Click Tools on the upper right, and the menu will expand with ways for patrons to refine their search.

CONSTRAINTS Size will be an important consideration. While image-editing tools can shrink or stretch images, monitors, print, and photographs have vastly different resolutions. Resolution means that an image file displayed on a TV screen is a different size in print, but rather than focus on trying to teach this, just advise the patrons to *always* look for the largest image.

If you click on Size, you can choose Large. If a patron will be printing the image, choosing Larger than

The default Google search bar, where refinements to a search can be made

is advisable. There they can specify 2 megapixels, or 2MP. The sizes below 2MP are screen resolution size for web use. 2MP is the first size that would in most cases be appropriate for print. Also, mousing over an image will display the size in pixels, (width by height). You can make the images default to always show this information by choosing More Tools in this submenu. Explaining pixels and resolution to non-technical people is normally the biggest stumbling block. The concepts may need going over several times, with the example of blowing up images to show artifacting (when an image becomes pixilated from being stretched to fit an area larger than the original image).

I suggest quickly covering how images that are one size in pixels are another size when displayed. My favorite metaphor for this is colored balls. An image is really a map for pixels, but think of pixels as colored balls—each pixel is a ball of a specific color. Monitors can build and show an image of 10 colored balls across, while print is using softball-sized balls, and video is using basketball-sized balls. So 10 ball images are larger in width when printed. Print and TV use the same map for the balls, but how this looks and its actual size changes.

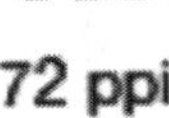

Different displays change the physical size of an image with a set resolution.

TYPES OF IMAGES The next option to teach is Type. These are categorized as Face, Photo, Line Drawing, and Animated. The Animated images will all be GIFs. Clip art, photos, and line drawings should be JPEG or PNG files (occasionally TIFF and GIF files too.) PNGs and JPEGs are both image files, but there are some differences. A PNG file is better for print or an image with text; JPEG is better for color reproduction. Only GIFs will have motion, but these can only be used in PowerPoint or web applications.

PRO TIP

Sometimes you will want an image that can be placed on a background, or without a background. If you are looking for an image that is not a box shape, meaning it has transparency so that only the item is visible (not the background), you will need to search for a PNG or a GIF file. PNG is the preferred file though. If it appears with a checkerboard pattern in the background, the checkerboard will not be visible.

USAGE RIGHTS The main feature you need to show the patron is the Usage Rights. The drop-down menu will provide these options:

- Not filtered by license: we do not use this, as it makes no distinctions on returns; it is the default state

The checkerboard pattern signifies a transparent area in an image.

- Labeled for reuse with modification: you can use and modify it
- Labeled for reuse: this is free to use it commercially but you cannot modify it
- Labeled for non-commercial reuse with modification: same as above but only for nonprofit or a non-business use
- Labeled for noncommercial reuse: same as above

At this point you can have the patrons conduct a search and see how the responses are returned. You will notice that filtering the results give fewer returns. Google relies on self-reporting for these filters; if an image is not labeled in any way (and most Internet images are not), it will not be returned once you apply the filters (a good thing to remember when you are tagging images). Of course, there is another side to this—some of those images that are returned may be usable, and the patrons may ask if that is the case. Remind them that the purpose of this class is to find images that they can legally use, and to learn that the way items can be searched with Google affects the returns. Many of the sites covered later in the class are not available to Google when it is indexing images.

As you move on, ask the patrons to click on an image; this will open an interface with other related images, as shown below.

It is very important that patrons understand that these related images do not have the same filter applied. They are related by content *only*, and there is likely to be items under copyright returned in that interface. I have often come across stock photography and copyrighted images in these returns when making a "labeled for reuse" search. Stress this fact to the patrons.

Copyright Primer

The information in this section should be reviewed in a PowerPoint or handout, although the patrons may have difficulty following it. Copyright is not a very interesting topic to cover, but it gives some context to why we search the way we do, and helps explain why we teach patrons how to search images that are free to use. The patrons should be made aware of how copyright works and why to make the effort to look for free images. I suppose it is worth taking the time to explain the possible repercussions of breaking copyright, but that would vary greatly on how and why the copyright was broken. Copyright is a complicated issue, and most situations are not always very clear-cut. This is further complicated by the fact that as librarians we cannot give legal advice. In the interest of not losing your audience or falling into endless what-if situations, it is best to just stay positive and explain when it can be used, while making resources available and being willing to discuss your level of knowledge after the class.

Explain to patrons that only in certain instances can they use commercial images. The most likely time is if an image has fallen into the public domain. Public domain simply means that the copyright for an image has lapsed. It may have been copyrighted once, but no one has extended the rights to the image past a certain built-in "expiration date" for the copyright. Some government images are actually released into the public domain. However, any images that were for intended for commercial purposes can have the copyright extended, so it is hard to say an image before a particular

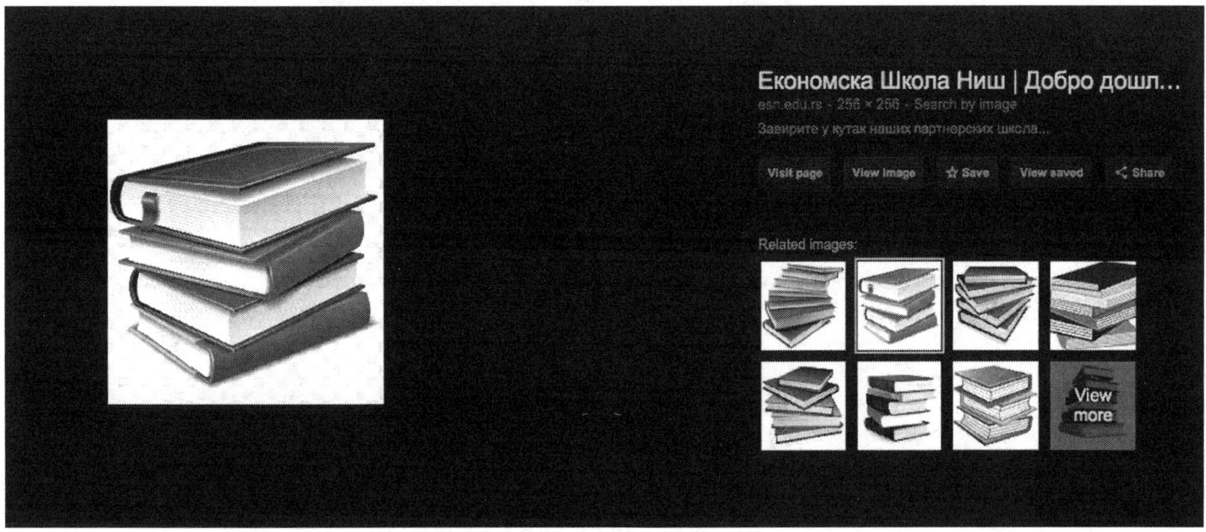

The related images in a Google search

date is definitely in the public domain. Luckily, some sites have done that research for us.

The other situation is what is termed "fair use." You can cover fair use, but of course we cannot give legal advice or necessarily tell them what fair use is for a particular image. If you feel the need, you can look up the actual fair use legal language. If you are tempted to skip this section, remember that they may hear of it somewhere else. Because the concept of fair use is used so often and the actual laws are vaguely worded, it would be a good idea to provide a description. Fair use can be broken down into two areas:

- Criticism, teaching, reporting, news, or research: images can be used for these reasons. In this case, the rule of thumb for fair use is whether the use of the work would interfere with the sale of or profitability of the work.
- Parodies, or other "transformative purposes": this one is trickier, since the work must be used for transformative purposes. The rule of thumb used by artists is that the work must be changed by at least 33 percent and in a new context. However, even that is incredibly vague. I would simply discourage patrons from doing this. If, however, you have an artist in your class, you can explain to them that they should research this topic, as it provides protection for his or her work.

Again, the world has changed a great deal since these laws were created. We have what is called a remix culture; we can scan, animate, and modify images in ways that were not considered when this law was created. The difficulty of navigating what is fair use led to what was basically a cavalier attitude toward copyright by website creators and bloggers, starting in the 1990s. The confusion and fear of litigation has led to the creation of Creative Commons (CC). Instead of punishing people for using images, people have made it simpler. The Creative Commons copyright system is used to clearly distinguish what and how something can be used. Whenever possible, look for objects copyrighted with the Creative Commons logos. We will later get to some sites that promote images copyrighted through Creative Commons.

What does CC mean?

LICENSES | TERMS

BY · BY SA · BY NC · BY ND · BY NC SA · BY NC ND

Attribution (BY)
Others can copy, distribute, display, perform and remix your work if they credit your name as requested by you

No Derivative Works (ND)
Others can only copy, distribute, display or perform verbatim copies of your work

Share Alike (SA)
Others can distribute your work only under a license identical to the one you have chosen for your work

Non-Commercial (NC)
Others can copy, distribute, display, perform or remix your work but for non-commercial purposes only.

The Creative Commons copyright legend

The Creative Commons logo is accompanied by the terms of use. This can be used to decide how, if, or in what context the image can be used. Share the diagram of CC licenses with your patrons and in the library (with proper attribution).

There are concise definitions of the licenses on the figure but I would add to these definitions:

- Attribution: this is pretty straightforward as a rule, but in practice, attribution can sometimes be difficult. Sometimes information on the artist is not as readily available as you would think. You may find an image that is four or five "shares" removed from the source. A good-faith attempt is usually enough, as long as you give some sort of information about where it was found.
- No Derivative Works: This license means you cannot modify the image. I do not believe this supercedes the fair use clause, but in the context of images, this means the image cannot be changed to alter the content. The most common understanding is when content is used for plays or written works. This license means that the written work cannot be turned into a video or film.
- Share Alike: Mostly important if your patrons want and can create derivative works. It simply states that any derivative works must be shared under the CC license as well.
- Non-Commercial basically means the user cannot sell the work, charge for its use, or use it to promote a product. Don't take some nice artist's cartoon character and put your dish soap in its hands.

Cheap and Free Images, Sounds, Video, and Fonts

Understanding Creative Commons means that patrons can now search sites that specialize in this license, like Wikimedia. You can call up a browser and take your patrons to that site and others where copyright-free images are available. The most likely outcome to the Google search is that they discover how hard it is to find a usable image when they apply filters. To encourage them to remain copyright compliant, you should give your patrons a little more help with other sites where they can get free images.

Most of these sites have simple interfaces and a simple link to start the download process. If you have gone over the Google Images search, then patrons should understand the basics of other sites. If you have explained copyright they should know why they shouldn't download from a stock photography site without a problem. They might also understand how "free photography and films" are often of too low a quality, or have a restrictive license. It is not uncommon to see a "free" stock photography site give away the low-resolution image and charge for the high-resolution image.

LIST OF GOOD SITES FOR FREE IMAGES

- https://commons.wikimedia.org/wiki/Main_Page: a site that is part of the Wikimedia group, searchable by subject matter through meta-tags. Again, there is no actual taxonomy, so it may be tough to find the right image.
- https://www.flickr.com/commons: part of the flickr photo sharing and hosting service.
- https://www.flickr.com/photos/britishlibrary/: A series of old images known to have fallen into the public domain.
- http://www.loc.gov/pictures/: Library of Congress images that are in the public domain.
- http://www.pdclipart.org/: public domain clip art. For the record, you will see a lot of clip art in the public domain.

LIST OF SITES FOR FREE SOUNDS AND VIDEO

- https://commons.wikimedia.org/wiki/Main_Page: a site that is part of the Wikimedia group, searchable by subject matter through meta-tags. Again, there is no actual taxonomy.
- https://archive.org: the Internet Archive, for sounds and video.

FREE FONTS Text can be a major part of an image, or an image itself. Patrons may wish to create a logo or flyer using a stylized font, so I want to add a note about free fonts, as this topic may come up in class. If you want to talk to your patrons about fonts, going over adding fonts, or downloading and installing them, would be a good idea. Fonts are fun to use, and provide a lot of bang for the buck in flyers and other print

A font can add Flair or CAN BE TOOMUCH

Fonts are best used sparingly.

applications. They are not very useful for applications. There are lot of free fonts out there.

I do suggest encouraging people to use fonts even if you are not teaching them how to do so. First of all, loading fonts takes some delicacy, as fonts come in different types, such as OpenType, TrueType, and PostScript. Also, a computer's operating system, (MacOS or Windows) may not support all these types. Fonts can also interact with a computer in a way that can create security issues. Most free fonts are safe; however, individuals often create free fonts, and they can be corrupt and cause issues, or even introduce a virus to a system. In general, I think you, as a librarian, should warn the patrons of this, and leave it to them to balance their own issues.

Icons are similar. In web design, custom icons can be very useful and have great impact. However, while they are surprisingly easy to make yourself, downloading an icon set could have some very serious security issues. If the patron knows how to repair those issues, that is great—go for it. If not, then you don't need to be the one who introduced them to the idea.

If you are asked about free fonts, here are the things to mention:

- Fonts must be installed; they are packages that interact with programs. This means they will be downloaded as a ZIP or TAR compressed file. They need to be uncompressed and then installed.
- Both Macs and PCs will actively help the patron load a font.
- If a patron chooses to download a font, it is worth the time to run it through anti-virus software.
- Do not be surprised if a downloaded free font contains errors, is corrupt, or does not support all text features (like bold or italics).

These two sites contain free fonts, which can be used commercially. You will need to use a search filter as you would with Google Images to restrict the returns:

- http://www.1001fonts.com/free-fonts-for-commercial-use.html
- https://www.fontsquirrel.com/

Google has also created fonts (https://fonts.google.com); they are an attempt to create consistency in web design. Google fonts are open source, meaning they are free to be used for free commercially, including web applications.

HOW THE TOPIC CAME UP AND BECAME A CLASS

Nothing was more annoying than running a class, say on HTML or CSS or even Microsoft Word, and asking people to pull up an image from Google to use. I always felt like I had to discuss copyright issues. It could bring the class to a screeching halt. In general, people did not care to hear anything about copyright or open source at that time; they were more focused on the topic of the class. Still, I knew that some of those people were looking for images for commercial use. I know looking the other way is "normal" for a church newsletter or a PTA bulletin, but we do have a responsibility to teach this information to patrons.

So, from those experiences came the idea for this class. Patrons generally want to use images legally, and understand that the effort to search for legal images was worth it. When this is taught, patrons can leave knowing a good-faith way to *not* break any copyright laws. Also, when teaching other classes, you will have the resources to tell them about using copyrighted material without delving too deeply into the issue.

Sell it Online—What Sells Where

Using Etsy and Redbubble

WHY BOTHER?

Libraries are central to the community as meeting spaces. As a public librarian, you are often the host for a local crafts-based club. Finding a way to support these kinds of clubs with technology can be difficult. An easy way to serve this demographic and promote your library's resources is this class on online selling. Selling on the Internet can be a good side career or even provide a main income. Compared to a brick-and-mortar store or selling to other stores, the profit per item can be significant. Add the ability to work from home, and online sales becomes attractive to many people. More importantly, it is a way to promote a crafts or art club and your local artisans.

WHAT PATRONS WILL NEED

- Basic computer skills
- An email account
- An image of something they would like to sell

WHAT YOU WILL NEED

- Some images with composition lines, and some to edit
- Ability to display an active computer screen (projector monitor, or enough room for everyone to gather around)
- An open Internet connection
- Some images of something a patron might sell
- Redbubble, Etsy, eBay, and FB accounts that can be accessed and deleted
- Access to an email account

IT WOULD BE NICE TO HAVE

- Measuring tape and a scale
- Some successful profiles from Etsy

OUTLINE

1. Which site is right?
   a. Creating for fun and profit
      i. Etsy
      ii. Redbubble
2. Setting up an account
   a. Etsy walk-through
   b. Redbubble walk-through
3. Attractive images and words
   a. Using Word to proof
   b. Shooting an image
   c. Creating a profile

THE BIG PICTURE

The focus on this class is making the patron feel comfortable selling online, helping them understand that different sites are for different goods, and giving them an overview of how to sell successfully online. The class can also help patrons understand that their hobby can be a good source of cash flow, and help them feel empowered afterward to be able to sell their goods. If you are not familiar with the websites covered here, you will need to review not just how to sign in, but also what kind of goods are available on each site. While you review the sites, it would be a wise idea to make some bookmarks in your browser of items or sellers you think would interest your patrons, or grab some screenshots of the actual sites.

CLASS

Which Site is Right?

First, a warning: not everything on these websites is "family appropriate." When you go to show the sites be aware of this, and be prepared. We cover two sites in this class, which are geared toward creativity compared to other selling sites like eBay, which is just a resale site. You do not need to run the class on both

> PRO TIP
>
> **Do you have knitting or quilting clubs at your library? Using this as an activity for one of those clubs is a way to do cross-promotion for library programs. Do you have a young adult or teen group that needs funds? Try creating a virtual crafts fair.**

types of sites; as always, judge from your audience. Also, this class calls for skimming over things like setting up an account, as it is geared toward people who should know how to do that from setting up email and other accounts. We will only involve ourselves in details unique to selling.

Creating for Fun and Profit

Walk your patrons though what the sites are used for, and their strengths.

ETSY Etsy is the home of handmade crafts. You may have seen or used or bought things from Etsy already. When you teach this program, it will be difficult to set up more than one or two people with a shop at a time.

REDBUBBLE Redbubble is similar to Etsy in the fact that it sells creative works. It is different in the sense that it only needs images. The actual physical item is the artists' works printed on items. These items can be:

- Clothing: t-shirts, scarves, and hoodies
- Stickers
- Phone cases
- Pillows and sheets
- Household goods: mugs, pillows
- Straight photographic prints

Setting Up an Account

ETSY WALK-THROUGH The trick to this will be to have ready-made accounts that you can use for instructional purposes. Understand that you cannot set up multiple shops, so you have two choices:

- Create a new account every time you run the class
- Set up a shop, and simply display the screens and walk patrons through adding items

In either case, everything will work until you get to the billing process. It costs 20 cents to list an item. If you do want to walk patrons through this process, they will be required to provide some very private information that you may *not* want to be privy to, so it is best to let them know upfront that they will need:

- Banking information, including routing and check numbers
- Valid credit card information
- Addresses and date of birth, and the final four digits of their social security number

You can show patrons the registration process for Etsy. They must provide three things to sign up for an account:

- email address
- Their real name and address
- A user name and password

Ask the patrons to bring images of their items for sale. Load these images to your demonstration computer. If they do not have images, you should have some placeholders available. Once an account is created, they are free to open an Etsy shop!

The first thing they will need is a shop name, which should either be descriptive or engaging. Again, I suggest using your own pre-created shop. However, as you are just starting the class, you can ask patrons what they are selling and what they would like to name their shop. Ask patrons what they think of each other's names; this would be a good way for them to solidify their ideas, rethink their names, or simply get everyone talking and sharing input.

Next, you will need to walk them through adding a listing. The listing screen looks like the one on page 85. Using one of the example images or one of the patron's images, fill out the form. Start by loading the image of the item and walk the patrons through the Title, About this Listing, and Category. Category will be important, because it will affect how people will be able to find the item to buy it.

Here is a good learning moment; does the item fit into one of these categories? If it does not, are they sure they want to list on Etsy? Items can definitely be shoehorned into one of these categories; for example, a calculator could be sold on Etsy, but the benefit of Etsy is the fact that the site is branded for homemade crafts. If it is not handmade, say the patron is selling an automotive part, then he or she will need to rethink the site. Or, if the patron's item is an image, then we need to go to Redbubble.

Once the patron has chosen a category, take a moment and open a second browser window to Etsy to browse that category. Look for two or three things, similar options, and their price point. You will notice that if you look at two or three items, you can gauge what the online price is for similar options, and use this to set your own price. Also look for the terms other sellers used in their Title and Category boxes. When you look for similar items, you will have seen some terms like Classic, Americana, Shabby Chic,

Photos

Add at least one photo. Use all five photos to show different angles and details.

Add a photo

Listing details

Tell the world all about your item and why they'll love it.

Title *

About this listing * Who made it? What is it? When was it made?

Category * None

Price * $

The Etsy listing is important to add a story and images to an item.

Select a category

- Accessories
- Art & Collectibles
- Bags & Purses
- Bath & Beauty
- Books, Movies & Music
- Clothing
- Craft Supplies & Tools
- Electronics & Accessories
- Home & Living
- Jewelry
- Paper & Party Supplies
- Pet Supplies
- Shoes
- Toys & Games
- Weddings

Etsy's categories are important to help buyers find a listing.

Upcycled, or Funky. Finally, look at the descriptions. See if any are funny or quirky. If patrons are doing their own searches, ask them to share the more interesting ones.

The next step is important. Once you have found similar options and noted the price range, click on an item and go to the bottom of the listing to Meet the Owner. Then click on Learn More About the Shop and Process.

A shop owner page will display the number of sales and, if you scroll down the left-hand side, the number

PRO TIP

You can preview and find some really good shops on Etsy, with a lot of sales and admirers. Some of these shops may also have a good story or profile for the owner. Share them as best-case scenarios. Remember to tailor the examples to your audience. I like katwise, at https://www.etsy.com/people/katwise. The owner started making upcycled "fairy coats" and they were so popular, she inspired a whole cottage industry of imitators—so popular, in fact, she was able to sell tutorials on how to make items.

of sales and admirers. Admirers and sales are a good gauge of the audience for their item. Ask the patrons these questions:

- How long has this person been on Etsy?
- Do they sell the same sort of thing the patron wants to sell?
- Do they have a large number of admirers?
- Do they have a lot more admirers than sales?

It they have low sales and admirers, but have been on a long time, they are not doing so well. If they have more admirers than sales, people like their stuff, but not enough to buy it. How is the patron's product different?

Leave any profiles in a new browser window open; we will return to profiles later in the class.

Going back to listing items, Title is the first question field to fill out. This is important because Etsy uses this information in search returns. Again, nothing about the listing is permanent until you submit it. Right now patrons can make any title they want, as long as it is fewer than 140 characters. It is also worth mentioning that a title cannot contain more than three words in all caps, or contain more than one instance of a special character. You can ask the patrons to refrain from making a title, as this can be a good guideline for whether there is a market for an item on Etsy. They can title an item later.

Quantity refers to the amount for sale. Etsy items are mostly single items, but it is possible to do a lot of items.

Renewal Options is important. Because your patrons are starting a shop, there is no way to know if something will sell. Tell them to choose manual, because this way they have four months; if an item does not sell in that time, they need to re-examine the market and their items. As mentioned earlier, Etsy charges 20 cents to list an item. For a few items this is probably not a major investment, but if they build up their shop, they need to know those items will eventually sell.

Type is self-explanatory, but if your patrons are selling digital items, they may want to explore Redbubble, before listing.

Description is important in two senses: It will be available for a Google search, and it is part of what sells your item. Writing a description at this point is *not* necessary. However, using a technique we have used in other classes, ask the patrons to describe their items to each other. While one describes an item, the other can write down what they believe to be key words or a short descriptive phrase. For instance, if someone is selling gold earrings in a hoop shape, you can use the phrase "gold hoop earrings" as well as "gold," "earring," and "gold earring."

Ask the patrons to set these notes aside, and we will talk about descriptions later in the class. Choose one of the patron's lists of terms for later, and hold onto it.

Section is the next option. When the patron has created a shop, they can divide the items into different sections. A knitter could create a hat, sweater, and throw section. Sections can also be thematic, so that same knitter could add a holiday section and put Christmas and President's Day sweaters there.

On the listing screen is a section on Variations; this is more for made-to-order items. Users must select a category and this will provide a series of standard variations to choose from. For instance, if you are knitting caps, variations could include size: S, M, L, and XL, or colors: red, blue, and white. Variations are not as important for people selling premade items, unless they are willing to let people special order items.

PRO TIP

By the time you reach shipping in a class, patrons will have been sitting for a while. It can be fun to get the patrons up and handle something physical.

A few items found in the library can be measured—a coat, jewelry, a book, a hat, or an umbrella. Use a tape measure and a scale if you have it, and use this as a time to talk about free shipping—this would make more sense for the jewelry versus the coat. Another point to bring up is foreign shipping options. Look at those expenses; are they prepared to deal with that cost?

Shipping

This section can almost be skipped. However, having worked with people who have run home businesses on Etsy and eBay I will share some rules of thumb:

- Let Etsy calculate your shipping cost on heavy and large items.
- Select a generous but not ridiculous processing time; you never know what will come up.
- Longer processing times can be offset by faster shipping options.
- For expensive items, include free shipping, and include the cost in your item's price.
- For small items or low-priced items, especially if they can order multiples, use a handling fee.

As far as setting a handling fee, there is a worksheet that Etsy provides so you can calculate your cost. The patrons may not need to use the actual sheet, but you will see there that time is covered. Patrons may not believe that charging for their time is important in this sense, but it is very important. A successful craftsperson knows that their time spent shipping is time not being spent creating another product. So, stress to them that maybe not at first, but at some point, time and the cost of shipping supplies will need to be calculated.

Search Terms

Search terms are how people find the item in conjunction with the title and description. Etsy is a little different, since these are broken into tags and materials. You will see tags again and again on sales sites. Materials are important, because Etsy is primarily a crafts site. People will search by terms like Cotton, Hemp, Recycled Wood, and so on.

At this point you can take out the lists of terms that patrons wrote about each other's items; if you choose not to do this, have an image ready and ask your patrons to describe it. Etsy will accept up to 13 search terms in Tags, and 13 search terms in Materials. Ask the patrons: Where do those terms fit? What phrases are most likely to get results? Now if, for instance, someone is interested in knitting, what terms other than sweater, yarn, and the color can be used? Ask patrons to come up with terms like cozy, or classic.

When you looked for similar items, you should have seen some terms like Classic, Americana, Shabby Chic, Upcycled, or Funky. These are useful terms to apply. If one description particularly stands out, like "round gold hoop earrings," then this is a description that can be repeated or used exclusively in the title (depending on how many terms a patron uses). If they can, add something applicable like Upcycled or Vintage, as this will increase the chances of the item getting viewed.

Warn patrons to be careful when they see a lot of a certain term; at one point, the term Steampunk was everywhere. Do not use a term unless it applies to the item. If you're making crocheted doll clothes, do not use Steampunk just because it is a common term. It will alienate buyers, and is against Etsy policy.

As far as descriptions go, have the patrons look at the terms again. You will notice that repeating the terms will not create a better search result. However, the description should include those terms. Instead of repeating them in sentence form, go back to the interesting items found. Do the descriptions tell a story? How are they more engaging that just a straight description? Is a wooden box being sold, or a box made from wood that a friend hand cut for them? Or a box like their grandmother had? These touches make a better description.

We already briefly discussed that patrons will need to set up billing, and why you do not want to do that in class. For this part, they will need an active checking account and a credit card. If they have ordered anything or paid a bill online, this should not be a problem.

They now have an Etsy shop. The final step will be to create a profile. This will be discussed later in the class.

REDBUBBLE WALK-THROUGH As we have gone through Etsy in so much detail, we can skim some of the similar parts. Specifically, the process for Title, Tags, and Descriptions are similar, as well as the final instructions for the profile.

Creating a Redbubble account is the same as creating a Facebook account. You will sign in with an email and create a password. Your account will also need a cover image. The image in this case must be 2400 pixels wide by 600 pixels high, in the JPEG or PNG format. This image is larger than the Facebook image and should be stylistically or thematically related to the art that the user plans to sell there.

The first step to show patrons is how to add artwork. If you click on the account icon in the upper-right corner, you will open a drop-down menu. On this menu is the option for adding a new work. The images must be in JPEG or PNG files. Luckily, these are the two most popular formats for digital images.

You should have an image ready to load, to show patrons what the final product will look like. If a patron asks what resolution an image must be, the answer will vary by product size. A product guide for images can be found here: https://help.redbubble.com/hc/en-us/articles/202270679-Dimensions-Format-and-Colour. However, we can simply say to people who are not full-time graphic artists that a t-shirt will require an image of at least 16-megapixels, or be around 4000 x 5000 pixels. Redbubble has larger items that require larger images, and many smaller images. The more important requirement is that the image has the right aspect ratio, meaning that the width-to-height ratio is ideal for the product.

If the concepts of aspect ratio and pixels are too intimidating to the patrons, Redbubble may not be the right venue for their work. Redbubble shows work by

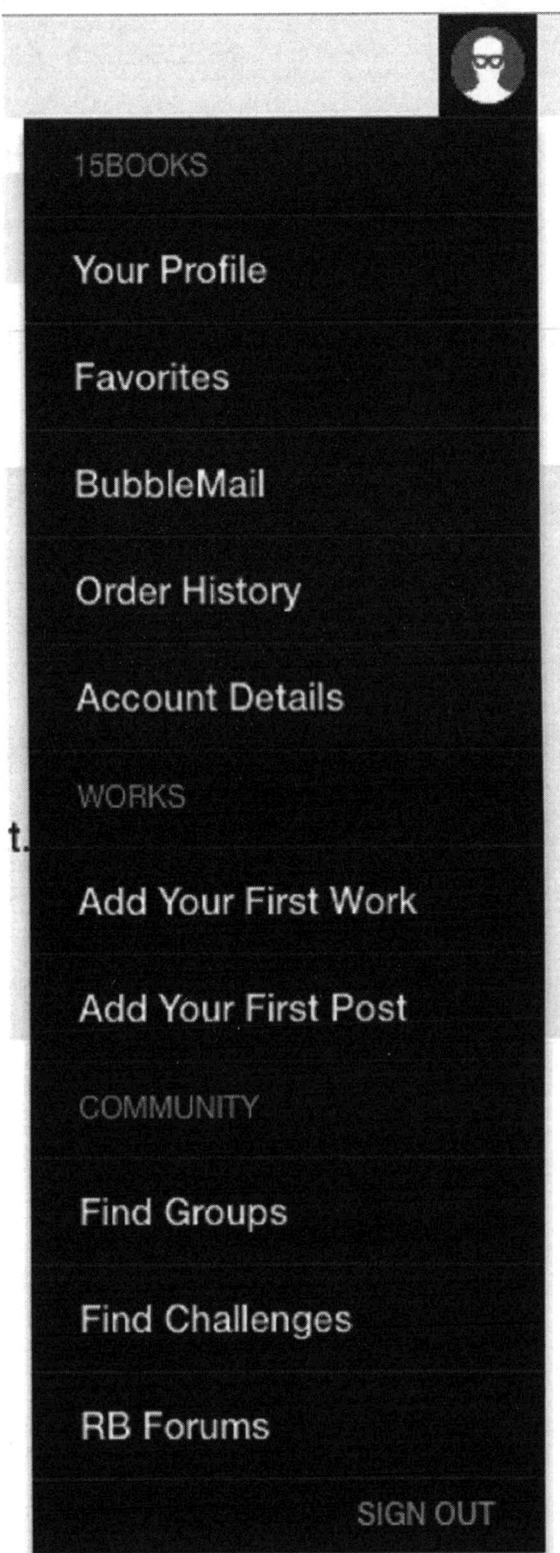

Redbubble's main menu is the first place to start an account.

some fairly serious artists. However, this is not to say that a watercolorist cannot scan in his or her work and sell it. Furthermore, Redbubble will not allow you to sell an item that does not have a large enough graphic to look good. So if your image is too small, you simply cannot sell that item. Some rules of thumb include:

- JPEG for colors
- PNG for text and detail
- The larger the image, the better
- Aspect ratio is important; Redbubble will allow background colors and tiling, but it can detract from the artwork

Once you have uploaded an image, you will be taken to the Product page. Here will be a list of all items that can be printed and sold.

PRO TIP

In this book is a class on PhotoCat (program 2). This program, with a scanner, can be used to resize and save images in different formats. If you have a large number of people who want to use Redbubble, that class can be combined with this one

The figure on page 89 shows the t-shirt on which the art can be printed. Each item can be interacted with separately. This is where you can adjust the size of the image, to make it fit on the product. You can also add a background color, and can tile an image that is too small or has the wrong aspect ratio.

If the proof does not suit the artist's needs, the item can also be removed from sale here. I suggest that any items patrons want to sell should be previewed and adjusted. It is important to note that the default for all products is enabled if a large enough image exists.

The ability to set your markup is also in the interface shown on page 89. Unlike Etsy, Redbubble will have a set cost, including a default markup of 20 percent. This cost includes everything, though, and your item is printed, shipped, and sent for you, so it is still a good deal. If, however, you would like to increase the chances of selling an item, the markup can be changed to a lower percentage. In addition, popular items, or storefronts with a lot of followers, can increase the markup for the items.

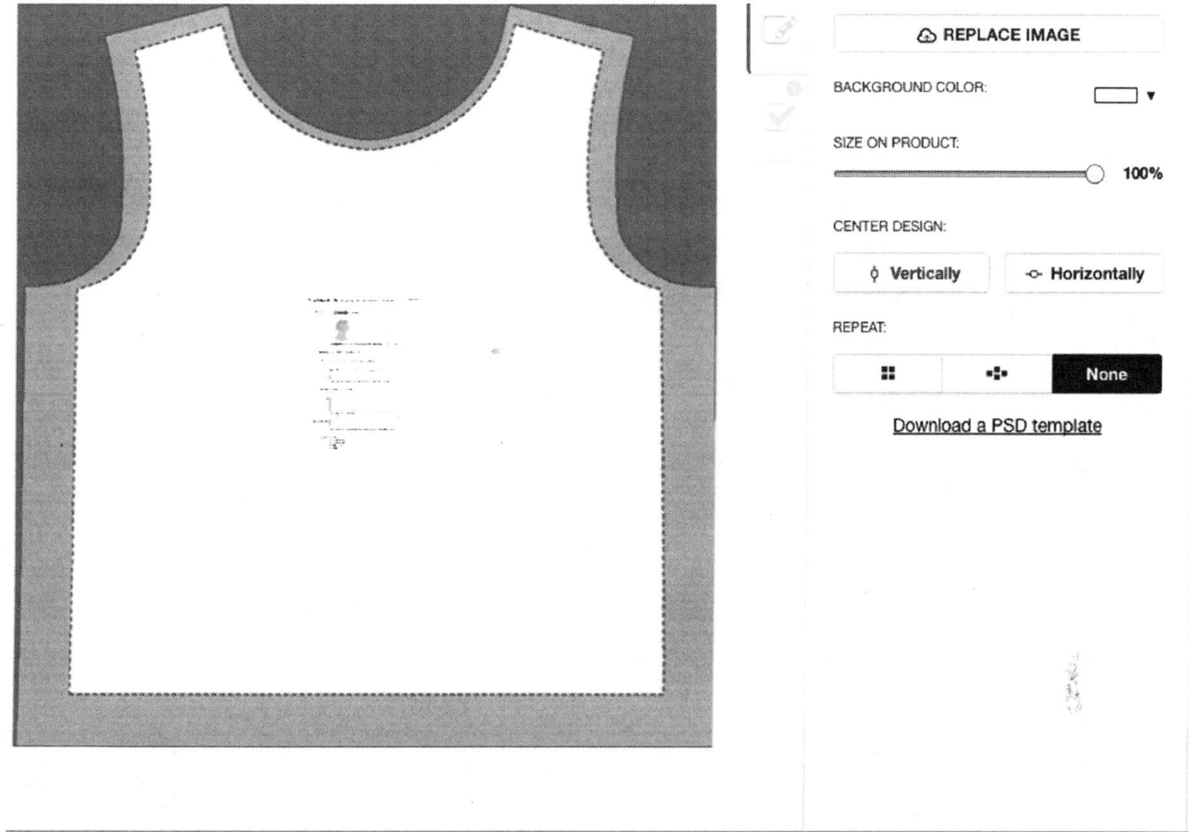

You can create a product with your artwork within Redbubble's interface.

Attractive Images and Words

USING WORD TO PROOF In the Etsy and Redbubble walk-throughs, we did not fill out the descriptions, but you should have called the attention to the fact that the description as much as the item is how things are sold. Let the patrons know that a good process for both is to get the tags. Organize tags by what is important, then string them together to create a description. A little story is more expected on Etsy; it doesn't hurt on Redbubble. Like most websites, text can be copy and pasted from Word. If your patrons did the exercise where they wrote key words for each other, make sure they have their notes, and tell them to string the phrases together at home. Place the tags in the *order of importance*, in Word or another text program, then string them together to tell a story.

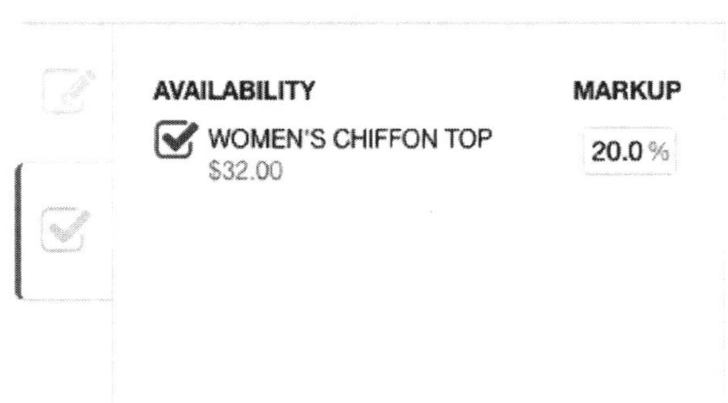

Pay attention to the Markup in the product interface; it can be modified.

SHOOTING AN IMAGE You will notice that on Etsy a lot of the images are "candid" shots, meaning photos are people holding things in natural settings. This is another opportunity to go back to Etsy and Redbubble—to look at some of the featured shops and their owners. Look at how they shot their images. Are people having fun with items for sale? Are these closeups of detailed work? In general, things that can be worn work well on models. Products sold on Etsy can be sitting in a pleasant natural background or in a neutral one.

When you look at the profiles of sellers, you can see that not everyone uses an actual picture of himself or herself. Those that do not will use something that either signifies a shop, or their product.

Look at the image of the shop owner of Emax t-shirts, on page 90. He managed to take a photo that promotes his shop with a product. I chose this image because I found it a clever way to promote and set a tone. If you look, you can find examples to share with the patrons.

emaxtees

14 Followers | 1 Following

An example of a clever use of the profile image

Your Public Profile Everything on this page can be seen by anyone

View Profile

Profile Picture Choose File No file chosen

Must be a .jpg, .gif or .png file smaller than 10MB and at least 400px by 400px.

Your Name David Folmar Change or remove

Gender Female Male Rather not say Custom

You must choose a city from the dropdown in order to have your shop appear in local search results. Learn more

City

Start typing and choose from a suggested city to help others find you.

Birthday - month - - day -

About

Tell people a little about yourself.

Favorite Materials

Share up to 13 materials that you like. Separate each material with a comma.

Include on Your Profile
- Shop
- Favorite items
- Favorite shops
- Treasury lists
- Teams

Etsy requires a seller to create a Public Profile. This is a chance to market your business as much as a product listing.

Creating your Profile

Using the images of shop owners, you can transition to the profile aspect of an account. Explain to patrons that the profile, like the description, is part of creating a story for the shoppers. Redbubble even suggests that you can choose an avatar, rather than a real image. The images on the profile are part of creating a sense of what the shop is selling. It does not mean a profile picture has to be "cool" or "sexy"; a picture of the shop owner's dog is acceptable, especially if that owner is selling handmade collars or leashes, or something else related to pets.

The rest of the information on the profile is self-evident. It is also nice to know that you can reserve the right to disclose information like age and sex on both services. What is important is the About blurb on Etsy, or the Public Profile/Short Bio on Redbubble.

You do not want your patrons to actually write this information during class. Instead, tell them to go to someone they like and respect and who likes their work. Ask them for four or five statements about them and their artwork. These statements can be strung into a bio in the same way the patrons put together the product descriptions.

If your patrons have shared work to sell, have them ask someone they admire to say something about the process and inspiration for three or four minutes. Then ask others to volunteer some statements for the bio. It is usually easier to let others toot your horn. It also creates some good will in the class.

HOW THE TOPIC CAME UP AND BECAME A CLASS

An old friend of mine named Mark, with whom I worked, made a decent amount of money on eBay as a side job back in its Wild West days, when it was only auctions run by real people, before businesses and resellers became so popular. He used his years of sales experience to maximize his profits. When I was working in the computer lab, we had a surprisingly large number of patrons selling on eBay. I ended up helping more than a few patrons by using tricks Mark had taught me—tricks like taking notes of other seller's tags and descriptions, and making the description a story. When I thought of doing a class on eBay, it seemed to me to be a little late. Multiple books on eBay and online selling had come out, and I was not sure I had anything to add.

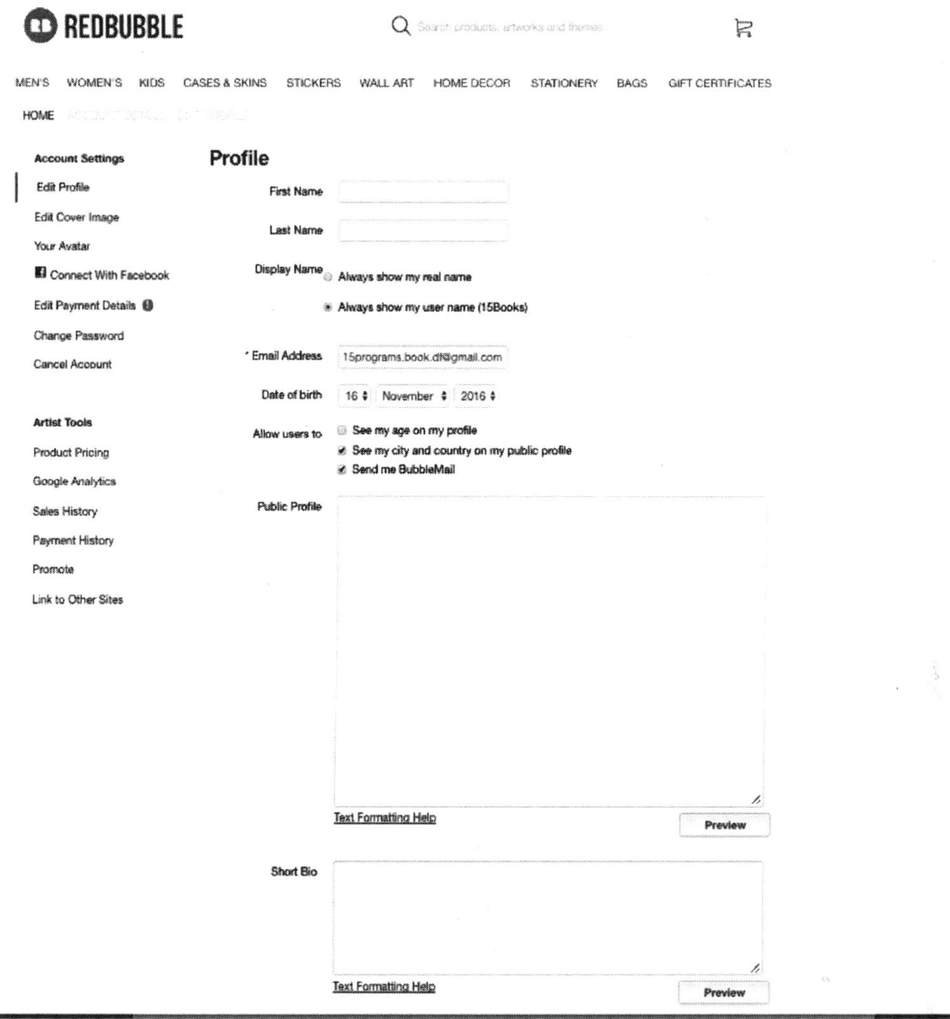

The Redbubble Profile Creation interface

> **PRO TIP**
>
> **Redbubble can be used in the same way a knitting class can use Etsy to self-promote and to promote the library. If your library has an anime club with people who draw, think of Redbubble as an outlet for their art, and include the library logo (with permission) and the club name. This is also a good way to turn graphics for special programs into t-shirts, without costing the library anything. You can simply set up the account and promote the shirt sales across your social media. The last idea is for libraries that may have visiting authors and artists, especially those writing for young adults. You might ask them to contribute something free, related to their visit (an image of a character in a book, or a drawing), to be sold on the online library shop. Both you and the artist get a mobile promotion that way, but more importantly, the shop serves to display the variety of events offered at your library.**

Then in my digital imaging class, I had an artist who wanted to know more about taking pictures of her paintings, so she could sell them on eBay. We ended up going over images of her paintings and discussing the benefits of selling them on Redbubble. This class was created based on Mark's advice for selling online, Mark's marketing knowledge, and the artist's needs, mixed with some great general advice for creating images and marketing. The class will always present a challenge, because artwork and crafts vary so much, but this general advice should do well.

Google Voice for a Home Business

Create a Virtual Office

WHY BOTHER?

When starting a home business, it is not a good idea to invest in anything more than you absolutely need. Luckily, Google provides some very powerful and useful tools for the home office. If you have patrons who are trying to start their own business, or working a "side hustle" (as freelancing is sometimes called), it is good to create some separation from your business and your life. Google Voice can help create that separation and save the expense of a dedicated phone line or cell phone. It also helps, especially in the case of a side hustle, to not take calls on an obvious second phone in your work place.

WHAT PATRONS WILL NEED

- Basic computer skills
- A Gmail account
- Cells phone if they want texts, otherwise a phone number to forward calls.

WHAT YOU WILL NEED

- A Gmail account
- Ability to display an active computer screen (projector monitor, or enough room for everyone to gather around)
- An open Internet connection
- A microphone
- Speakers connected to your computer

OUTLINE

1. Setting up Voice
   a. Creating a Gmail account
   b. Choosing a number
2. What does Voice *do*?
   a. Explaining Google Voice features
3. Forwarding calls
   a. Forward to cell
   b. Forward to text
4. Set up a Voice box
   a. Recording a message

THE BIG PICTURE

A library is supposed to help its community, and traditional activities based around the humanities and book readings are a great way to do that. As we look to grow as institutions, a great place to expand our efforts to empower people is small businesses. I know law librarians who do series of classes on making your company and the legal aspects of running a business. Computer and technology savvy can be helpful, too. Google Voice can help patrons make starting a business much more cost effective. It is just putting them in touch with a resource they might otherwise not know about or think to use in this way.

CLASS

Setting Up Voice

Voice is part of Google's productivity suite; Google offers Google Docs, G+, YouTube, and Google Voice. You can even use these tools to create a virtual office if you buy your own domain name. However, all of this relies on actually having a Google account. If the patron has one, great—it makes life easier. If they do not, then we need to get that out of the way. I am sure your library has run a program on making email accounts, but I will summarize the steps here.

CREATING A GMAIL ACCOUNT First, make sure that your patrons can receive text notifications. It will be important they do. Now open Gmail. When patrons are on the log-in screen, they can make any name they want. It is important to stress that they will not have to disclose this email when using voice. It is possible to use a private email account, just as it is possible to use a private phone for Google Voice. If, however, they do not have a "professional email account," it would be good to kill two birds with one stone.

The log-in screen will ask for a name. It only accepts A–Z, 1–0, and a period (.) as entries.

Be careful not to get tied up in this step, as way too often when creating names for email accounts, the preferred name is taken. Just add a period, followed by phone (.phone) to any user name your patrons come up with; rarely, they may need to add a number as well. If they try to get creative or specific, it can take time to find something unused. Let them know that this user name does not need to be shared with potential clients.

Next, Gmail will want the full name, birthday, and sex of the patron. Try and encourage them to use real information, as this can be important if they use this account in other ways. Then Gmail will ask for a cell phone number. It is important they give a phone number that is accurate and matches the cell phone that they brought with them. When they try and use the account, Google will use text notifications to activate and check the account.

Choosing a Number

Now you can set up a Google Voice number. Again, it is important that patrons have a cell phone handy. You can walk them through these steps to get the Google Voice account set up.

1. First, make sure they have an email account. Everyone should have them at this point.
2. Simply Google search Google Voice. You can log in with your email credentials.
3. Google will ask users if they want a new number or want to use their mobile number. We will choose "I want a new number." While it is possible to use call forwarding, voicemail transcriptions, and notifications with an existing number, part of the process here is to create a separate phone identity for the patron.
4. Google will ask for the phone number again. Theoretically, a home line can be used, but for this class, they will need a cell phone handy, as Google will ask you to verify this number. You can explain to your patrons that this number does not have to remain the forwarding number, as it is easy to change or add numbers later.
5. Make sure the patrons are set with their phone and explain to them that Google is going to give them a two-digit number to verify their phones. When Google calls, have everyone enter their two-digit number to verify. Don't worry if they do it incorrectly at first—they can retry the number, or get a new one easily.
6. Now is the time to choose the actual phone number they will use. Google will ask for an area code, zip code, or geographic location. Google would like to provide a local number; take advantage of this, and use the local area code. When an area is chosen, Google will provide options of numbers in that area. Have the patrons choose a number, and the first step is done.

PRO TIP

When we cover call forwarding for Google Voice, the actual physical phone and its number can change. Although this class is for small business use, people who, for whatever reason, may change phones often (homeless, economically disadvantaged, or without a phone plan), can also use Google Voice to create a permanent contact number.

What Does Google Voice Do?

Patrons should have questions about what they can do with Google Voice. It is a very rich tool for calls. First, it is toll free inside the United States and Canada, and can make cheap international calls. But most important, it can also be accessed from any computer anywhere, including inside your library, so users can check messages and send texts from any computer that has Internet access. If the computer has a microphone and speakers, they can even make calls from it.

Messages can also be forwarded to other phones or multiple phones, and Google can send a text or email when a message is left. Maybe most impressive is the fact that Google Voice can *transcribe* the voicemail to text for you, although, in my opinion, patrons might not want to rely on the accuracy of the transcripts for business concerns.

The figure on page 95 shows the Google Voice interface. Notice that you can change the Google number. Forward to Google, or forward text messages and receive voicemail notifications as texts on your phone.

Also notice that the menu on the left side has:

- an Inbox for your voicemail
- an Inbox for texts
- call history
- hidden from view, the ability to view recorded calls

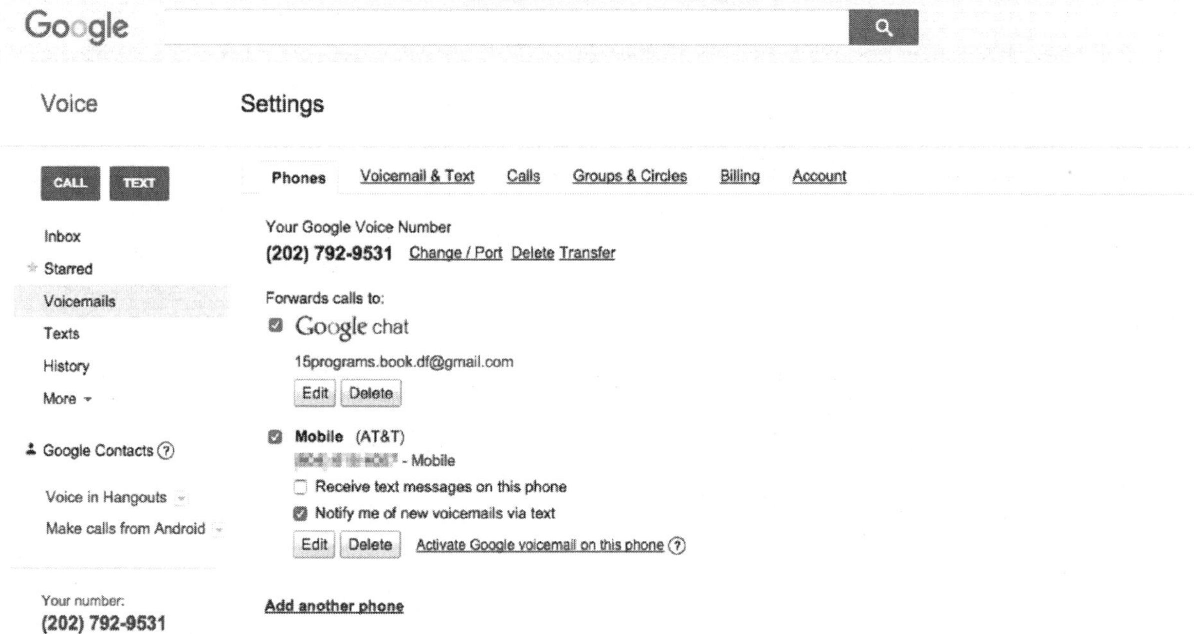

The main Google Voice interface for creation of a Google Voice number

Google Voice can record phone calls, but it is up to your discretion to point this out. I suggest avoiding this because you could get lost in conversation about privacy concerns.

Below Google Contacts are two features: one is to make calls in hangouts, and the other will allow calling directly from a phone. This option may be confusing; if Google Voice does not call directly from a phone, how does it call? Look at the top of the menu on the left again to find out.

At the top are two buttons, Call and Text. Text will bring up an interface, which you can use to make texts from your computer screen. Texts go out through Google, and responses will show up both in the computer and on the phone where you forward the Google Voice account. Call will bring up the interface pictured on the right.

Opening this interface will give you the option of making a call from Hangouts or your mobile phone. You dial the number you wish to connect to, and it rings through to your phone, then dials the number you called and connects it to your cell phone number.

The question that patrons may have at this point is. what does Google Voice *do*? If it is not capable of making calls *directly* from your phone, how can it be used? Well, it can make calls, if you use an app. However, the real benefit of Google Voice is its ability to *answer* calls and *forward* the calls from the Google Voice number.

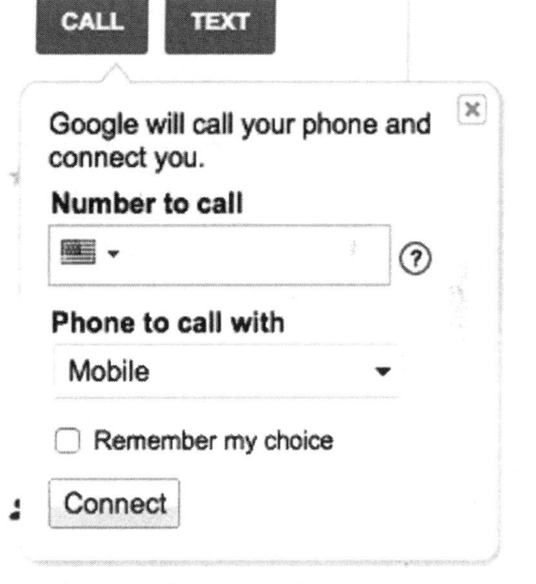

Google Voice calls can be connected through your cell phone.

Forwarding Calls

Have your patrons open Settings under the gear icon in the right-hand corner. Under Phone, you will see that users can choose where to forward their calls. The Google Chat option (which works with Google Hangouts and certain third-party applications) can be loaded on a phone, and used on there.

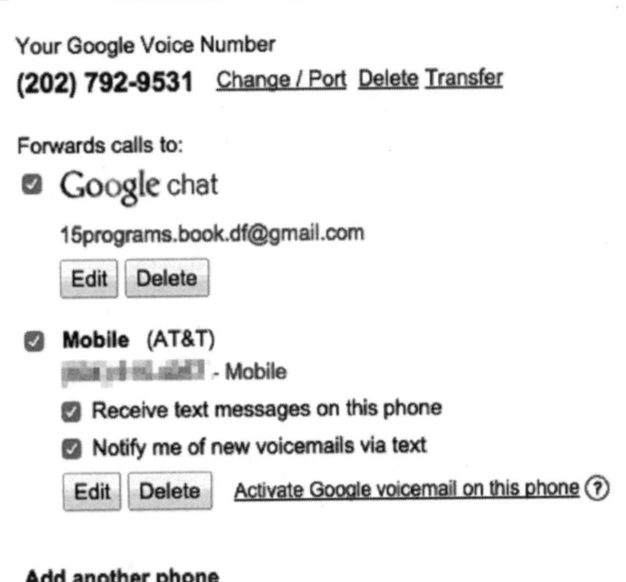

Google Voice calls can be answered on your phone or set to notify you by text.

More importantly, you can choose to have your smartphone receive texts and text notifications of new voicemails.

Patrons can also navigate to the advanced settings by clicking on Edit, and then on Advanced Settings. Patrons can transfer the calls on a schedule, and send them to voicemail. The schedule can even be customized to send voicemail at certain times of the week or day, or to send voicemail to one phone at one time and another phone at other times. In this way, patrons can control when they are available, not unlike having office hours for their virtual office.

Another important feature is the ability to transcribe texts.

If you have the patrons navigate to voicemail and texts (see the figure on page 97), they will see that there is a check option to have Google transcribe voicemails. Again, I would state that transcription is not highly accurate. However, it can often to be useful to have an idea of what a call was about, and for this class, it allows us to have some fun with the patrons.

Since the patrons now have Google Voice accounts and cell phones with them, have them call each other, leave messages for each other, and let them ring through to voicemail and leave each other voicemails to see how funny transcription can be. They can see how text notification and voicemail works, and how they will get four options with a call:

- Answer the call
- Send it to voicemail
- Send it to voicemail and listen in real time
- Answer and record the call

This will be a great time for patrons to ask questions and try out the functions while you can guide them and others can help.

Setting a schedule of when to answer Google Voice calls creates separation between your private and personal calls.

Phones Voicemail & Text Calls Groups & Circles Billing Account

Voicemail Greeting Record New Greeting System Standard Play
This is the general voicemail greeting callers hear

Recorded Name Play Record new This is the name callers hear when they call you

Voicemail Notifications Alert me when I have new voicemails
Email the message to: 15programs.book.df@gmail.com Add a new email address

Text Forwarding ? Forward text messages to my email: 15programs.book.df@gmail.com

Voicemail PIN ? New PIN
Confirm PIN

Voicemail Transcripts ? Transcribe voicemails
Allow automated Google systems to analyze your voicemail messages to help improve transcription quality

Save changes Cancel

The option of transcribing voicemail messages allows patrons to check calls in their browser from any device.

Set Up a Voice Box

The final step is setting up a voicemail message. This is really not necessary during the class, as it will be impossible for them to record all at the same time. However, a voicemail message will be necessary for them to have a fully functional "virtual office."

Under the Voicemail and Text tab, there is the option to Record New Greeting (see the figure on

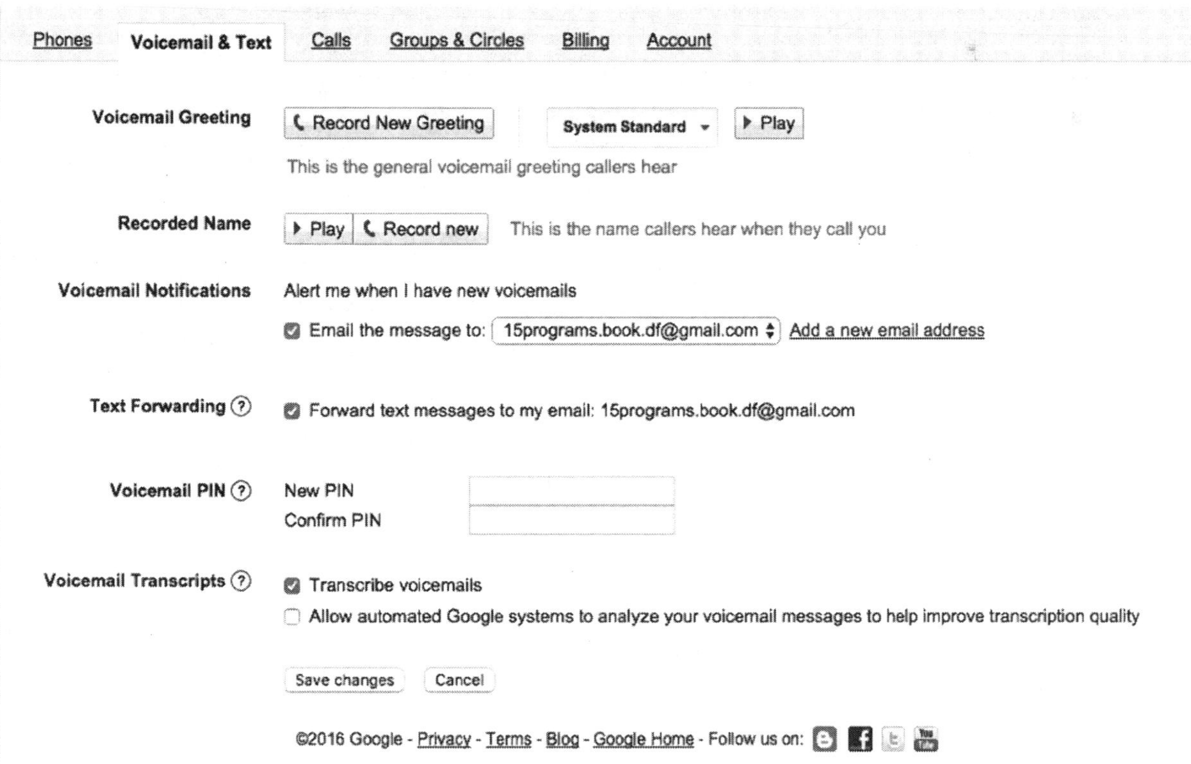

A customized greeting on Google Voice will help create a sense of professionalism.

page 97). When recording a message, Google calls the mobile phone used to set up the Google Voice number. On this phone, you can record a message. If you have time, you can suggest that patrons record messages for each other; now they have virtual secretaries, instead of just answering services.

HOW THE TOPIC CAME UP AND BECAME A CLASS

As mentioned earlier, Google offers a full suite of productivity tools. I know of people who have created Google Docs classes and I have heard of these being used to replace Microsoft Office. A patron who had worked in IT came in using Google Voice as a virtual house phone for homeless people. It was ideal, as these people could communicate and apply for jobs and, most importantly, check for calls. While many homeless shelters will allow their clientele to get mail there, phones calls were problematic. Even if the shelter could take a call for you, then a potential employer would know the applicant was homeless.

The class was originally designed for homeless people, and it can still be taught that way. I thought, however, that orienting the class toward small business owners or home workers would have a more diverse audience and be useful for a wider range of libraries.

PRO TIP

Does your library have media lab? You can use it to record messages for patrons' new voicemail accounts. You will need to create a Google Chat account and call the number from their account.

1. **Record a voicemail message in your editing software.**
2. **Go into your Windows Sound settings (right-click the speaker icon in your Taskbar or go through Control Panel), and select Recording Devices.**
3. **Change your Recording Device to Stereo Mix (or Line In). Now that your Windows Recording Device is set to Stereo Mix, whatever plays from your media player will be channeled in place of your microphone.**
4. **Go to Google Voice Settings > Voicemail & Text > Voicemail Greeting.**
5. **Open Gmail and be ready to answer a call from Google Voice.**
6. **Click on Record New (in Google Voice) and select your Gmail Google Chat phone. Answer the phone when it rings.**
7. **When Google instructs you to record your message, play the recording in your audio editing software. It goes through Stereo Mix and records to your Google Voice voicemail.**
8. **When you are finished, remember to go back to your Windows Sound settings and change Stereo Mix back to Microphone.**

If you have a microphone, display this, and bring a sign-up sheet for the media lab or audio booth. Not only will you get more people to use your media lab, you can promote that it is used to help with economic growth as well as artistic development.

Show Them to Sell Them

Easy 3D Programs for Contractors and Interior Designers

WHY BOTHER?

Contracting is one of the easiest startups and sidelines for people. The problem is that the skills needed to be a contractor are not the same as what is needed to sell the client on your ideas, or effectively communicate them. 3D software can help in these cases. If librarians can teach patrons how to use a 3D printer, we can teach contractors how to make a 3D house. Interior designers can also use 3D software to create a rough walk-through.

WHAT PATRONS WILL NEED

- Basic computer skills
- Ability to download software from the web

WHAT YOU WILL NEED

- A copy of Sweet Home 3D for your computer or lab computers
- Sweet Home 3D Textures library downloaded
- Sweet Home 3D Furniture library downloaded
- A floor plan and a 3D model to work with
- A thumb drive, or have patrons bring their own computers

OUTLINE

1. Finding, loading, and opening Sweet Home 3D
2. Creating a room and base plan of the design
   a. Understanding the tools
   b. Building walls, windows, and doors
   c. Using primitives to create architectural detail as part of a base plan
   d. Customizing rooms with textures and finding custom furniture libraries
   e. Arranging and moving furniture
3. Creating views and a walk-through
   a. Changing lighting conditions for effect
   b. View your room and save a view
   c. Creating a walk-through

THE BIG PICTURE

You can show patrons how to create rooms and layout in Sweet Home 3D, and then create images and walk-throughs to show their clients. You will help them find the program, show them where to get resources, and orient them to the features of Sweet Home 3D.

CLASS

This class is different from the other Sweet Home 3D program in this book (program 4), as your patrons should come with a much better grasp of how to use the software. Viewing floor plans should be something familiar to them, and the actual addition of detail is not as important as creating the views and modifying the objects.

Finding, Loading, and Opening Sweet Home 3D

Sweet Home 3D is free software, and can be found at http://www.sweethome3d.com. It is a site maintained by the owners, and it can also be used online at that website. I think it is worth the effort to download the software, but for instructional purposes, you can simply use the online program because it is platform independent, running on Windows, Mac, and Linux operating systems.

On the Sweet Home 3D home page, you will find links to custom 3D models and textures. If patrons are so inclined, they can also use the free 3D furniture editor, but other free furniture libraries can be imported to Sweet Home 3D, meaning there are thousands of models to choose from (including plants and people models to use as decoration). While this may not give decorators an exact match, they can at least give a decent impression or feel for what they are going for.

We are assuming that the patrons will have some computer experience, so it's possible that just showing them the site and providing a handout will be enough to help them know where to find the program without walking through the download process.

Creating a Room and Base Plan of the Design

UNDERSTANDING THE TOOLS In the other Sweet Home 3D workshop, we covered making walls and rooms in detail. This audience should have more familiarity

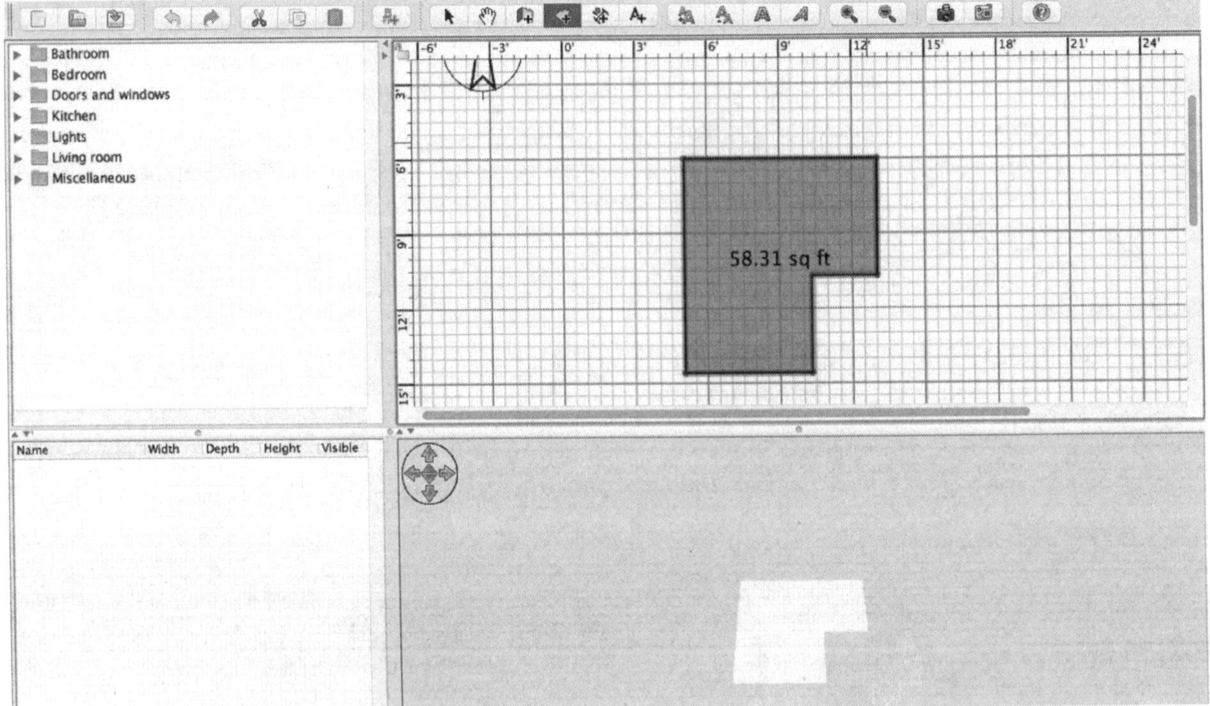

The main interface of Sweet Home 3D, where a room can be designed

with architectural plans, so we can just discuss the interface.

The first thing to do is open Sweet Home 3D. If you provide the computer, have it preloaded. When the screen opens, you can see that it is divided into four areas:

- Left top pane is the library of items, or furniture catalog
- Right top is the design area, or Home Plan
- Below that is the Home 3D View
- The remaining area is furniture and items to add

The toolbar across the top is where you can select actions to take. Mousing over the items will display their functions. The toolbar is broken into six areas. First are the File functions (Save, etc.). Next is the Undo/Cut/Copy/Paste area (normal keyboard shortcuts work with this program). These functions should be familiar to the patrons, and you can gloss over them; the rest I suggest going over in detail. The next two sections are Add Furniture, and Plan Tools.

From left to right are:

- Selection tool
- Grab or Move tools
- Create Walls
- Create Room
- Create Dimensions: useful for making ADA-complaint hallways, or setting aside space for traffic flow
- Add Text: good for labeling aspects of a room for patrons. The next four boxes are text modifiers:
    - Scale Up
    - Scale Down
    - Bold
    - Italic
- Zoom In
- Zoom Out
- Create Photo
- Create Video

If the patrons have access to computers, have them create a room. It would be best to have them

The Sweet Home 3D toolbar

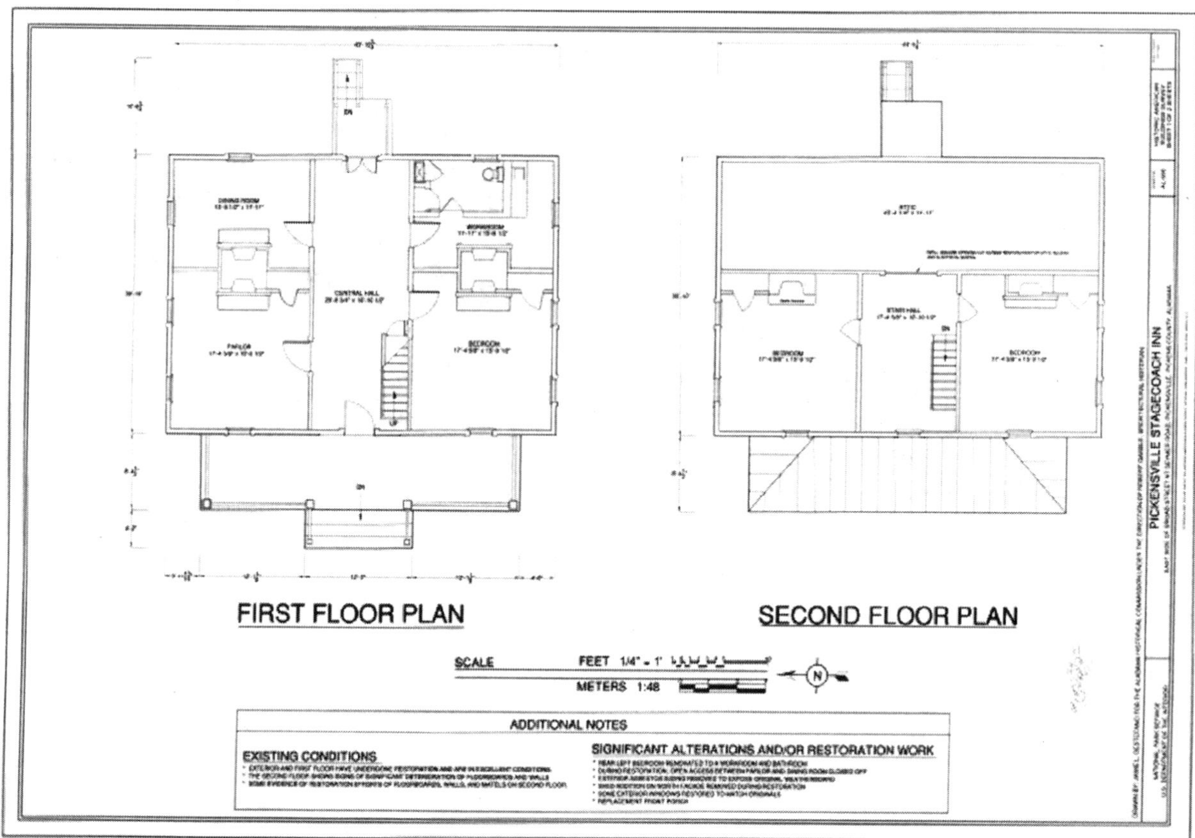

A floor plan from Wikimedia Commons, useful for recreating rooms in the Sweet Home 3D program

all use the same specifications. The best way to do this is project is with series of measurements for real rooms, including doors and windows. Measurements can be found on the Wikimedia Commons (https://commons.wikimedia.org). Pictured above is an example of a simple floor plan I chose by Jaime L. Destefano (in the public domain), via Wikimedia Commons.

BUILDING WALLS, WINDOWS, AND DOORS The room design is simple, and even without exact measurements, it should be possible for contractors or interior designers to create a good approximation of an actual room. The goal is for patrons to focus on the creation of a real room, not creating a room. Of course, any variations they would like to add is up to them.

Have them use the Create Room tool to approximate a design. The actions for using the Create Room tool and Create Wall tool are as follows:

1. Choose the appropriate tool.
2. Move the mouse to the grid area of the program.
3. Click to create the first anchor point.
4. Position the mouse to the next anchor. Anchor points can be added by clicking.
5. You can create irregular shapes and rooms by adding multiple anchor points.
6. When adding the last anchor point, double-click.
7. Double-clicking on an existing anchor point will exit the room creation.

You will use almost exactly the same process for walls. Walk your patrons through this process, displaying it for them. Do not feel the need to create a functional room to display. Patrons should be encouraged to play and explore how to use the tools. At this point they only need to learn the process.

Be warned that the Home 3D pane will fill with the room and walls as the patrons build them. Encourage them not to be distracted by it yet.

At this point, the patrons should have an empty room in which to place doors and windows. They can follow the placement of the windows and doors. The process will be almost the same for placing furniture. In the Furniture library or catalog in the upper left pane are a series of categories. The third down is the Door and Windows drop-down; open it, and a variety of door and window styles are available. Display for the patrons the process of placing a door.

PRO TIP

Since you are working with contractors, it is possible that they will have existing architectural plans.

1. **Click on Choose Image and choose your image in the file dialog box. Sweet Home 3D supports BMP, JPEG, GIF, and PNG formats**
2. **Once the image is loaded, click on Continue.**
3. **Define the scale of the image by moving the end points of the colored line drawn in the image in such a way that this line matches a known length. Then type the real length of this line in the Length of the Drawn Line field, and click on Continue.**
4. **Define the origin of the image in the plan, that is, the point in the image matching the point (0,0) in the Home Plan. Then click on Finish.**
5. **Once the Wizard is closed, your image will appear behind the Home Plan grid at the chosen scale, as shown in the figure on page 100. If you chose the wrong scale or location, edit these by choosing Plan > Modify Background Image out of the menu.**

You can go to http://www.sweethome3d.com/examples/userGuideBluePrint.jpg for a tutorial and to use a provided blueprint.

1. Click on the door and drag it to a wall. It will auto-center into the depth of the wall.
2. Now double-click on the door in the Home Plan; this will open the Modify Furniture interface.

Compared to the patrons in the class for redecorating with Sweet Home 3D, hopefully these patrons will be at ease with the Modify Furniture window. Location and size are the only two parts of this interface you will need to go over in the class.

You should also drag a box from the Miscellaneous menu, and show patrons the Miscellaneous interface.

PRO TIP

Not everything patrons may need is provided in the interface. For instance, there are no flat-screen TVs or computers provided. You have dragged a box to the Home Plan, place a second box, and use the dialog to raise it to the height of the first box. By manipulating the width or depth, you can create a stand-in for a computer or flat screen and cable box. Using the Furniture menu, you can group the items together. Now they can be moved as *one* item.

The points you want to stress are:

- The Mirror icon will change a door's direction
- Checking Keep Proportions will scale an item when you change one measurement
- A window or feature can be elevated, or walls can have their width changed.
- If you have a specific piece of furniture or art, you can name it in this dialog box and display that name.

CUSTOMIZING ROOMS WITH TEXTURES AND FINDING CUSTOM FURNITURE LIBRARIES Usually by this point, someone will have comment on how bland the 3D version of the room looks. I have heard it called a dollhouse, plastic land, and a padded room. Download some of the furniture models and textures from the Sweet Home 3D website to spruce it up. The furniture libraries available on the site are more interesting than the default set with the program. Also of interest are other 3D models created in programs like Blender, which can be imported. Sweet Home 3D will accept models in the OBJ, DAE, and 3DS formats, and it is possible to find free models online. Especially in the case of TV, stereo, and other devices, there are many to choose from. You may even look for new ones. The best thing about the 3D printer revolution is that more and more sites are popping up every day.

If you do not import new furniture, or even if you do, take the patrons to http://www.sweethome3d.com/gallery.jsp. Here you will find 3D models that are rendered by people who have worked in this program for a while. It gives patrons a taste of what is possible. You can also open a browser and go to http://archive3d.net/ and show them some of the models that exist at other locations.

After showing the patrons what is possible, show them how to make changes to what they have. They may be able to make their own furniture options. Open the Modify Furniture dialog, preferably for a wall. The two bottom sections of the dialog box are Color and Shininess.

1. Click on the Color Radial button.
2. Now click on the box next to it to call up the Color Picker.
3. Select a color from either the swatch or HSB interface.
4. The wall (or furniture) selected is now that color.
5. In the case of the wall, Shininess can be used to represent paint types—Matte for flat, or Shiny for satin finish.

The texture element of this interface can be problematic. It does not display particularly well on a computer monitor, but open it anyhow and show the patrons how it changes the object.

1. Select the wall again.
2. Click on Texture.
3. Now click on the box next to it to call up the Texture Picker.
4. Select a brick or wood texture and click.
5. The wall is now brick.

PRO TIP

Texture can be loaded from images in either the JPEG or TIFF format. If your patrons are inclined, do a simple Google Image search for large textures. Find what texture they are looking for—wood, brick, or even wool. These can then be imported. For a really interesting effect, import a picture of a person or place, and use that for a texture. An image placed on a box object makes for quick original artwork for a room.

It is difficult to get good results on a monitor for the default textures. This can be addressed by uploading texture libraries. Some can be addressed by using furniture models that have better textures than the default furniture.

Now you need to show the patrons how to move the furniture for a good arrangement.

1. Click on the Select Object tool from the toolbox.
2. When you click on an item, you can drag and drop it anywhere on the Home Plan view.
3. You can also nudge the furniture using the arrow keys of the keyboard.
4. When an item is selected, you will see the rotation arrows (the arrow in a circle—do not confuse this with the straight arrows that affect the dimensions).
5. You can also rotate an object in the Modify Furniture dialog box using the angle value in the Location section.
6. If you need to place an object, like a houseplant or TV, on another item, look at the height of an item in the dialog, and set that as the elevation of the item you are placing your object on.

At this point, you can let the patron play around for a while creating rooms; this is a good way to break up the class time. If you are more inclined to move ahead, the Sweet Home 3D site has some completed rooms. Preload these to the computers, and have the patrons open and modify them.

Creating Views and Walk-throughs

NAVIGATING THE HOME 3D VIEW The default view is aerial of the Home 3D View. The other option is Virtual Visit, which shows the room as seen from a person in the room. First explain to patrons that the Home 3D View be modified with the mouse. The green arrows in the corner of the view will:

- Zoom in and out
- Rotate the view
- Change the elevation of the view

Ask the patrons to play with this view in their models, or demonstrate it for them. Select the 3D View menu, and select Virtual View on this menu. Select this, and a wireframe person appears in the Home Plan box. The Home 3D View is now from the perspective of that person. The green arrows in that box now control the person's rotation and tilt. The arrows can also be used to zoom in and out. If you wish to view the room from a different position, you can use the Selection tool to move the person, just like you move the furniture.

VIEW YOUR ROOM AND SAVE A VIEW Let the patrons play with the top view option, move their person, and look at the room from different angles. You can explain to patrons that this view in itself is worthwhile for the purposes of displaying a room to a client. With this you can show a layout and change it, and display those changes from the viewpoint of the person. The ability to make "live changes" is a benefit of loading the Sweet Home 3D software on a computer to show a client.

The benefit of creating a photo or a walk-through is better resolution. Here are two images created at the default resolution, compared to two high-resolution photos created in View. The Sweet Home 3D User Guide has examples of rooms rendered in both low and high resolution. I have taken some high- and low-resolution images from their user guide (http://www.sweethome3d.com/userGuide.jsp) to give you examples, shown below.

You can see that there is a huge difference in resolution. Unfortunately, very large photos take a considerable amount of time to render. However, small ones can be rendered quickly to show your patrons, and for your patrons to demonstrate to clients. For the class, just make low-resolution images so that you don't end up watching the computer "think." To create a photo:

1. On the toolbar, click on the Create Photo tool. The Create Photo dialog box will open.
2. The image on the side shows you the default.
3. Click on the Create button on the bottom, and the same image as the Home 3D View box will appear in the window.
4. This image saves as a file to share with clients.

The patrons will want to impress the client with their images, so to make these more impressive, you can increase the size of the image. The better the image, the easier the plan is to sell, so demonstrate for the patrons how to do that.

1. Change the width and height to at least 1200 × 750 pixels; even larger is better. However, the larger the image, the longer the render. The 1200 × 750 size should display well on a monitor.
2. Move the Quality slider to Best.

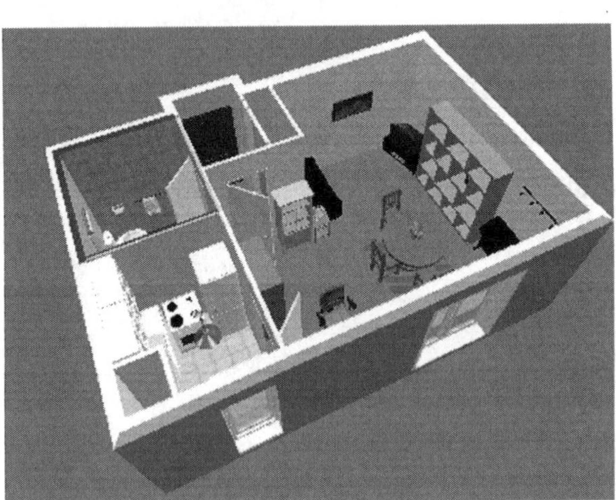

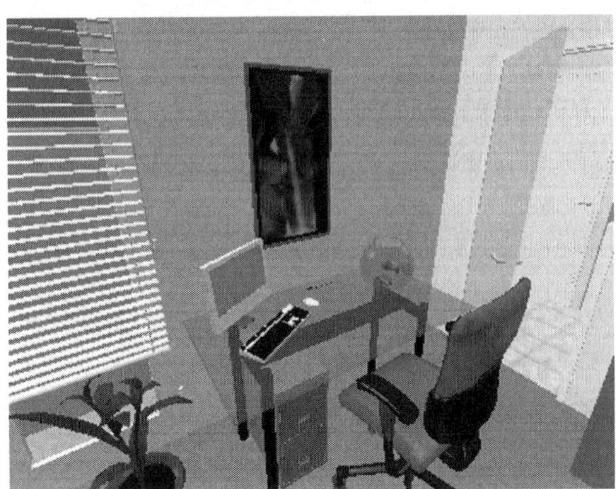

High- and low-resolution images from Sweet Home3D

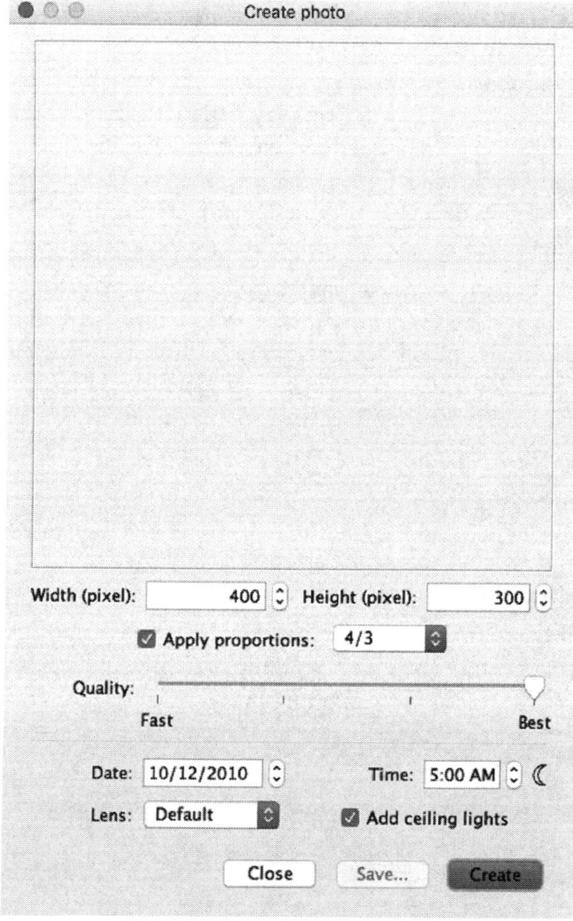

The Image Creation interface

3. The dialog box will change, with new options at the bottom. These will affect the quality of light in a room.
4. For a warm-looking room, change to a summer date (between the months of 6 and 8). And keep the time as daytime.
5. For a more dramatic look, check on the feature Add Ceiling Lights, and set the time to night.
6. Now you can render the image. It may take a few minutes; ask the patrons to open their programs and create some photos while waiting for the render.

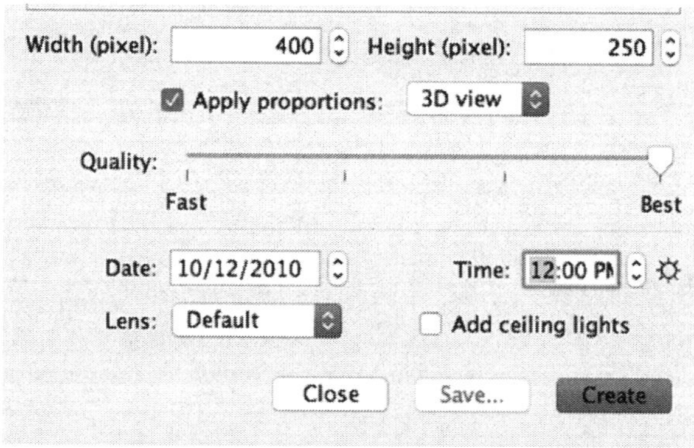

Quality controls resolution in this interface

These photos can be sent to clients through email, or displayed on a monitor.

While still in the low-resolution Virtual View, have the patrons try different views and angles of their rooms to get a sense of what is possible.

CREATING A WALK-THROUGH Under the Home 3D View menu there is an option to create a virtual walk-through. In this case, the largest size is 1920 x 1080 pixels, or standard high definition. I would suggest having a video ready to play; there are some on the Sweet Home 3D website that I referred to earlier.

The process for a walk-through video is similar to Create Photo. The difference is the time. Sweet Home 3D will control the timing. If you need a character to move slowly, you must only make small location changes between key frames. Do not change the size or quality settings for demonstration purposes. Obviously, the patron should use the better-quality setting for clients, but video renders are slower than photos. Now walk your patrons through this process.

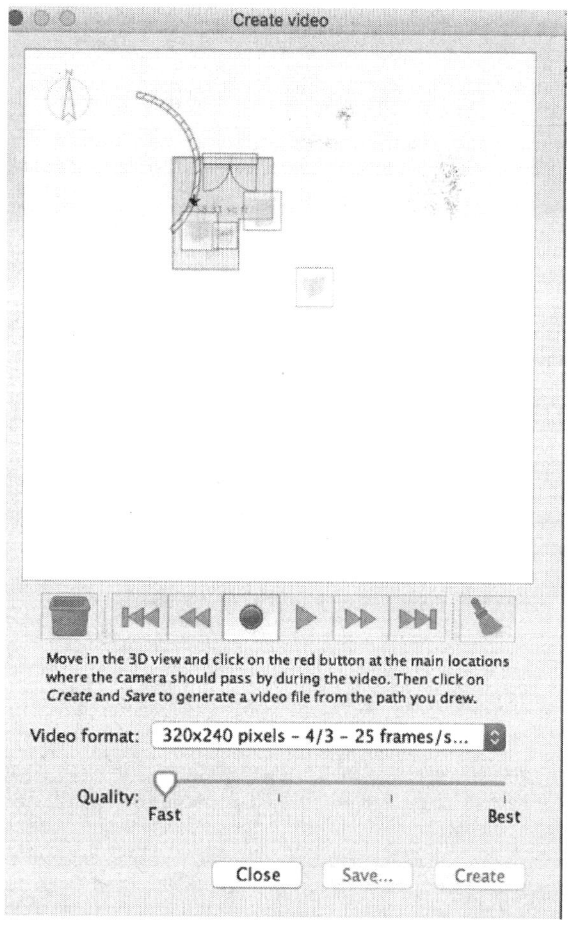

The Create Video "walk-through" interface

1. Click on Create Video in the Toolbar.
2. The Create Video dialog box opens.
3. Move the person to a starting position; it should be at a doorway or outside the room
4. Click on the red button (for added impact, click twice).
5. Move the person in the Home Plan box.
6. Click the red button again.
7. Repeat until you have moved the person through the room.
8. Call the patrons' attention to the Home 3D box; this is where the video will display.
9. Click Create.

The video will display in the box, but the timing may be off. You will need to save the video and open it with a media player. The patrons have some similar functions with the Create Photo and moving the view. They should be able to quickly create their own videos. Give them some time, and then ask them to share their videos with each other.

HOW THE TOPIC CAME UP AND BECAME A CLASS

Originally, I used this program with teens and tweens in combination with video game design and LAN gaming. The kids understood the interface easily enough, but were not sure what to do with it. When the library I was working for at that time was discussing some renovations, I thought that instead of just talking, I could use this to show my ideas. The interior designer who was volunteering to help us asked about the software, and indicated that her students could use something like this. She ended up being the first "class" for this program.

I thought it would be a good idea to offer a class to people who wanted to try 3D creation without getting into computer-aided design skills. I have noticed that many times, older contractors will send other office staff to take computer classes. A secretary or bookkeeper may show up to see what it is about. It is helpful to keep links to schematics of actual plans from the Sweet Home 3D website to show that this software can be a serious as well as fun tool to use.

Claim Control of Your Online Reputation

Google, Bing, and Yelp Your Free Web Presence

WHY BOTHER?

Librarians understand that part of helping our community will be helping small businesses in it. Social media and web presence are part of the reality of business today. When Yelp and Squarespace hit the scene in the early 2000s, these created a boom for the businesses that were able to use them. While that boom is over, people do tend to look up reviews and information online. It is information that not every business owner understands how to interact with, or even to find.

I know small business owners who struggle with their online presence. The choices they had were to hire someone to manage their web presence, contract with an agency to do it, or do it themselves. While this is more of a seminar than a class, it will teach your patron the basics so that they can make an informed decision and have a better understanding of what to do, or what they would be paying for if they hire someone to do this.

WHAT PATRONS WILL NEED

- Nothing

WHAT YOU WILL NEED

- Ability to display an active computer screen (projector monitor, or enough room for everyone to gather around)
- An open Internet connection

OUTLINE

1. Where are you on the web?
2. Claiming search engine listings
   a. Google Places
   b. Bing
3. Google and Apple maps
4. Other options
   a. Yelp
   b. Angie's List
   c. Merchant Circles

THE BIG PICTURE

You will walk patrons through a basic Internet search for a company. Talk about the sites on which they can find their company listing, and how they can take control of that listing. Then you can talk about best practices to maintain a healthy web presence.

CLASS

Where Are You on the Web?

Start by asking patrons what their businesses are. Are these brick-and-mortar? Contracting? A home-based business? Brick-and-mortar, or a business with a physical location, is usually the easiest to find. It is possible that a contractor or home-based business will *not* show up online. For some people this might be okay, but does not guarantee that a business will *never* show up on the web. Google, Bing, and other search engines don't just maintain the information; they pull their information from aggregators. These aggregators do not always provide accurate information.

Ask the class if anyone has had a problem with inaccurate information, and ask him or her to share that experience. If no one has had that experience, you can explain to your patrons that it is possible for business owners to control their own listings, correct inaccurate information, add information and pictures, and answer bad reviews.

> **PRO TIP**
>
> **Most of these sites can easily be claimed, but you may not want to try and expose the information from a live site to the patron. Simply log into Google, Bing, and Maps Connect and create a faux business to demonstrate.**

Claiming Search Engine Listings

When people search online for a business, the first site they will encounter is a search engine. It is easy to make sure your business shows up in the results of a search in your area just by claiming the information on the search engines. Google and Bing both have their own services for showing local businesses.

Google Places

The first step for the patron will be to Google their business. Make sure to search using both the name and location. The listing should show up in results.

- If it shows up, under address and phone is a link, Own This Business. Follow the link to take you to the Add your Business page, and auto-populates the information.
- If the business does not show up, go to https://www.google.com/business/ and sign in. Then choose Add your Business. If you add your business, you will have to fill in the business information. Make sure to check whether you make deliveries or service people at the location. This will affect how the business shows up in search results.

In either case, the business owner will need to verify the listing. There are currently two ways to verify, by mail and by phone. By mail may take up to two weeks in some cases; verification by phone is only available if the listing was *already active*. Phone verification has a problem with navigating phone trees, so if your phone is answered by a service or messaging system, Google's verification system will simply state the verification code; it cannot dial an extension or wait for an answer.

Once you have verified your listing, you can:

- Add or correct the address
- Add or correct the phone number
- Add or change hours
- Add a website
- Add photos

Bing is almost identical. The major difference is that you will search on Bing, and if it is not found, you can go to http://bingplaces.com and sign up. There you can search for your business as well, or create your

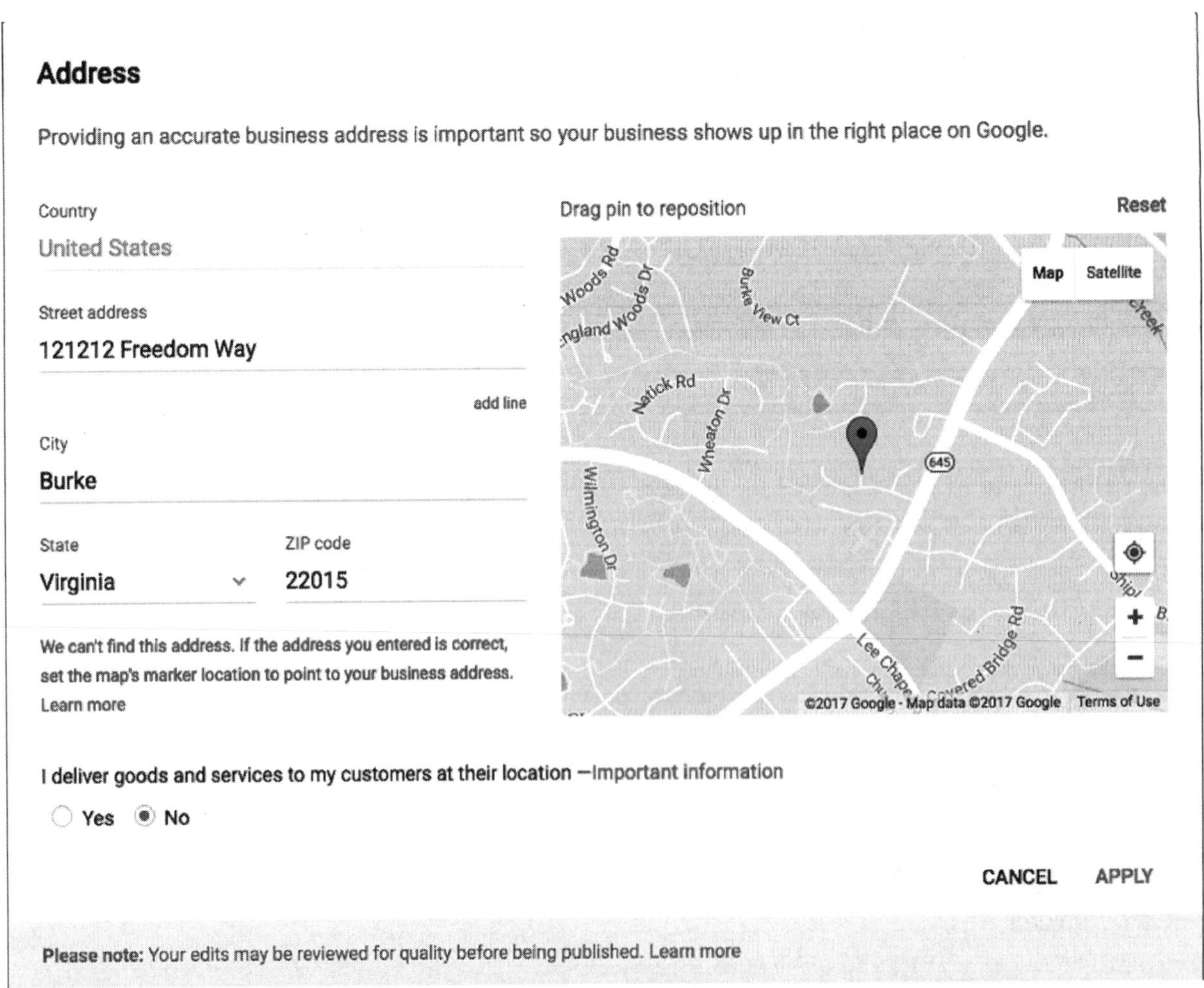

Patrons can be found on Google Maps by claiming their listing on Google places.

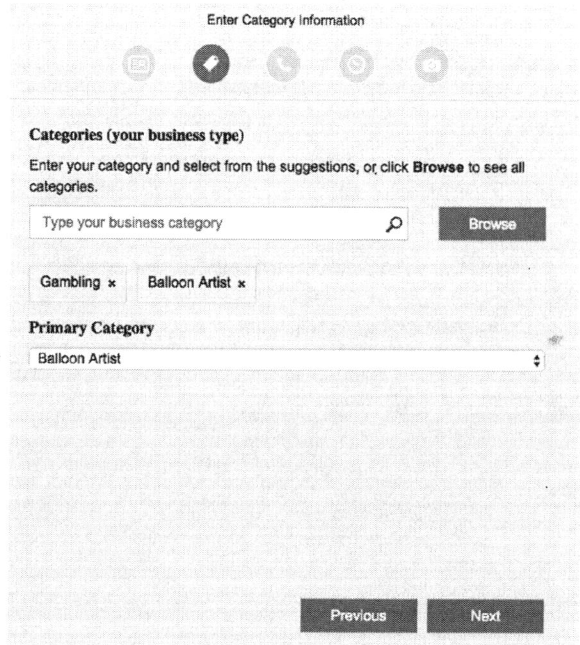

Categorization is always important for making a listing searchable.

business. The interface is a little more complicated. If you claim or create your business, you can:

- Correct or give an address
- Correct or add a phone number
- The interface for Categories allows you to add tags
- Add contact information for email, Facebook, and Twitter
- Add business hours
- Add photos

Google and Apple Maps

When you claim the Google place, your business will be added to the Google map apps. Additions to Apple maps will have to be done separately. Go to https://mapsconnect.apple.com/ and log in. Search for your business. If it is found, they owner can claim it like Google and Bing. When a site is claimed, the process is almost identical as those for Google and Bing. The major differences are:

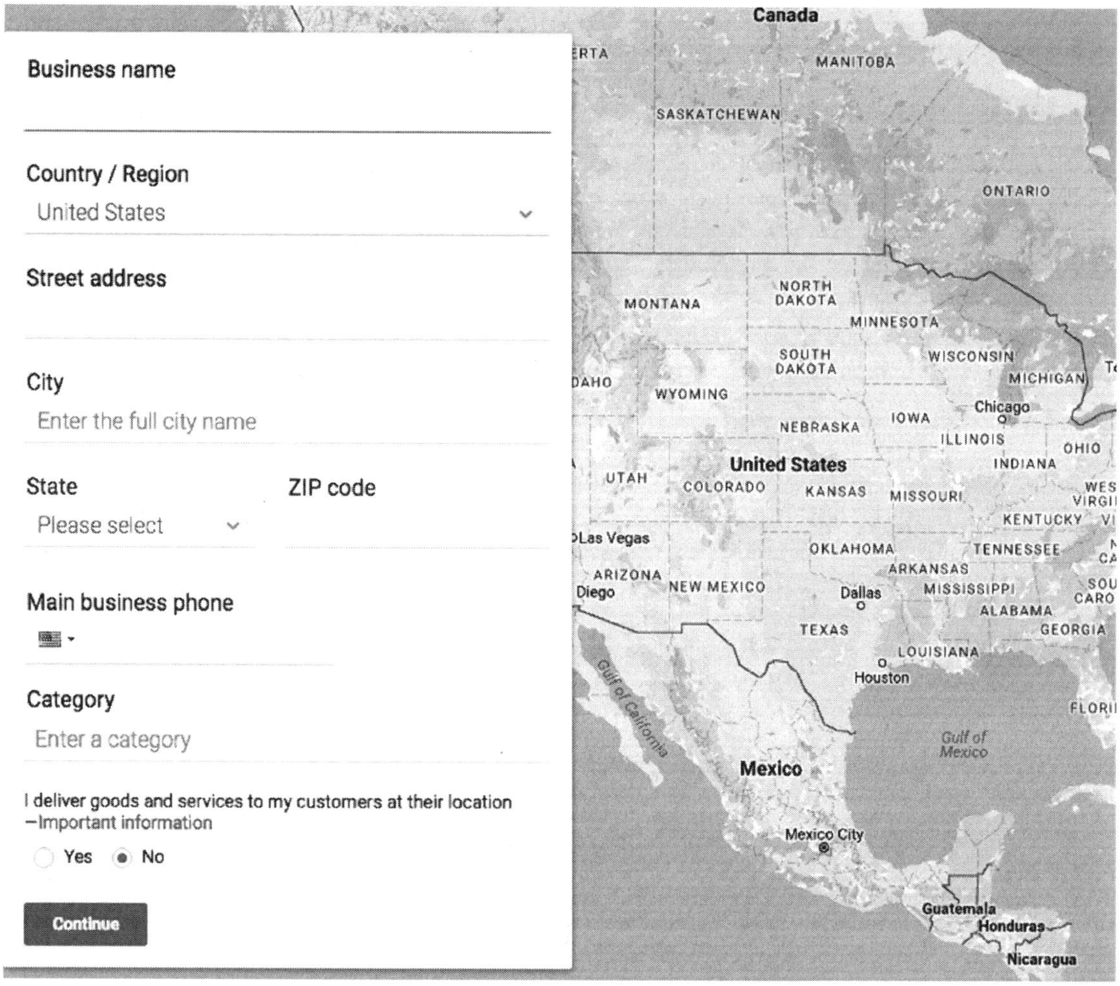

Business name
Country / Region
United States
Street address
City
Enter the full city name
State
Please select
ZIP code
Main business phone
Category
Enter a category
I deliver goods and services to my customers at their location —Important information
Yes No
Continue

Bing places are almost identical to Google places in terms of claiming a listing.

- You can link to Yelp
- You can attach an app that is sold on iTunes
- You can identify whether you accept ApplePay
- You cannot add images

At this point, your patrons' businesses can be found on both major GPS apps on smartphones.

Other Options

There are other services that may be important for patrons to search. These are more focused on types of businesses. Examples are:

- Yelp: for restaurants and clubs
- Angie's List: for contractors, home services, and doctors
- Merchant Circle: for small businesses and especially business-to-business merchants

The decisions to sign up for these should be made after the patrons search to see if they are listed, and if their competitors are listed. However, they should always claim a listing on a site if there is a review, which leads us to the best practices:

- Claim a site if information is wrong, at least to correct it.
- Claim a site if there are bad reviews.
    - Always answer a bad review, not with hostility, but apologize and offer to make it better.
    - Do not get your friends to add reviews. People notice if there are suddenly great reviews for a place, within a small time frame.
- If there is a specialized site, consider joining it.

HOW THE TOPIC CAME UP AND BECAME A CLASS

In another life, I was a communications and marketing contractor. I worked mostly with computer- and web-based jobs, and the technical side of the jobs. However, contractors get stuck with odd duties. One of my duties was claiming sites for a client. I had to research sites and look for reviews every two weeks, and help the client address those reviews. When I became a librarian, I noticed that whenever we ran a social media class, there was always a small business owner trying to understand social media marketing. More often than not, they had not claimed the basic listings on Google and Yelp, an activity that I know people would charge a lot of money to do for them. So, I pulled together the major sites for businesses, noted how they have changed and their best practices, and put them together in a short, easy lesson.

Index

About the Author

David Folmar has twenty years of digital video and audio production and presentation experience. He was an early adopter of digital technology, starting with his first TI-80. David worked in the Richmond Public Library system as a digital literacy librarian and then as emerging technology librarian. During that time, he became involved with the Richmond maker community and game development community.

In 2016, David moved to the Northern Virginia area. He now researches user experience design (UX), social media, open source software, gaming and simulation, digital and media literacy and is currently working with children's STEM programs in robotics, coding, and digital design. As a librarian, he has spoken at computer and library conferences, and has a book published by Rowman & Littlefield on using gamification as a community engagement tool.